ACHIEVING IMPACT IN RESEARCH

SUCCESS IN RESEARCH

The Success in Research series has been designed by Cindy Becker and Pam Denicolo to provide short, authoritative and accessible guides for students, researchers and academics on the key area of professional and research development.

Each book is written with an eye to avoiding jargon and each aims to cut to the chase of what readers really need to know about a given topic. These are practical and supportive books and will be essential reading for any students or researchers interested in developing their skills and broadening their professional and methodological knowledge in an academic context.

ACHIEVING IMPACT IN RESEARCH

EDITED BY PAM DENICOLO

Los Angeles | London | New Delhi
Singapore | Washington DC

SAGE

Los Angeles | London | New Delhi
Singapore | Washington DC

SAGE Publications Ltd
1 Oliver's Yard
55 City Road
London EC1Y 1SP

SAGE Publications Inc.
2455 Teller Road
Thousand Oaks, California 91320

SAGE Publications India Pvt Ltd
B 1/I 1 Mohan Cooperative Industrial Area
Mathura Road
New Delhi 110 044

SAGE Publications Asia-Pacific Pte Ltd
3 Church Street
#10-04 Samsung Hub
Singapore 049483

Editor: Katie Metzler
Assistant editor: Anna Horvai
Production editor: Thea Watson
Copyeditor: Rosemary Morlin
Proofreader: Louise Harnby
Marketing manager: Ben Griffin-Sherwood
Cover design: Shaun Mercier
Typeset by: C&M Digitals (P) Ltd, Chennai, India
Printed and bound by CPI Group (UK) Ltd,
Croydon, CR0 4YY

Library of Congress Control Number: 2013934432

British Library Cataloguing in Publication data

A catalogue record for this book is available from the British Library

MIX
Paper from
responsible sources
FSC® C013604

ISBN 978-1-4462-6704-2
ISBN 978-1-4462-6705-9 (pbk)

DEDICATION

For all the researchers who strive to make a difference.

CONTENTS

LIST OF BOXES, CASE STUDIES, FIGURES AND TABLES

BOXES

CASE STUDIES

FIGURES

TABLES

ABOUT THE CONTRIBUTORS

EDITOR

Pam Denicolo is a chartered psychologist, recently retired from her full-time role at the University of Reading where she developed the Graduate School system and the post-registration professional practice and research element of the School of Pharmacy. She maintains there a research group focussing on PCP approaches to research. She continues to provide workshops for doctoral students and supervisors worldwide and has also taken up a part-time appointment as professor at the University of Surrey, advising on Doctoral Training Centre development and other matters pertaining to doctoral studies derived from her membership of national committees, advisory boards and working groups.

Her passion for supporting and developing graduate students is demonstrated through her contributions as Vice-chair of the UK Council for Graduate Education Executive Committee, as Chair of the Society for Research into Higher Education Postgraduate Network and Executive Editor of the Guides for Supervisors Series, and as a member of other national committees and working groups which, for example, review and evaluate the impact of the Roberts-funded generic skills training, and the concordance of UK universities with the European Code and Charter. She was a key contributor to Vitae's development of the Researcher Development Framework (RDF) and the QAA's Doctoral Characteristics Advisory Group and its revision of the Code of Practice section on postgraduate research.

With her colleague Cindy Becker from Reading University, Pam co-edits and contributes to the Success in Research book series for Sage.

Contributors

These were drawn from the RCUK/Vitae Impact and Evaluation Group and contributors to the UKCGE Impact Workshop at the University of Warwick, February 2012.

Tony Bromley is responsible for the Graduate Training and Support Centre (GTSC) at the University of Leeds, which is part of the university's Staff and Departmental Development Unit. GTSC provides personal and professional development activity for postgraduate researchers across the university. He is also the advisor for Vitae in the Yorkshire and North East region of the UK and Associate Editor of the *International Journal for Researcher Development*. With a PhD in Materials Science, Tony worked in industrial research and development and postdoctoral work before following his interests in the professional development of researchers. He then held researcher development posts at the University of Manchester before returning to Leeds in 2006 and his current role. He was author of the UK sector evaluation impact framework for researcher development (see www.vitae.ac.uk/impact) and has continued in a leading role during the implementation of the impact framework, also authoring subsequent sector reports on the evidence for the impact of researcher development. He has presented widely and facilitated many workshops on the researcher development impact framework. He has also published in the materials science and education fields (consult his personal university webpage http://www.sddu.leeds.ac.uk/sddu-tony-bromley.html).

Colin Chandler was employed by Northumbria University as Postgraduate Research Advisor and Reader in Rehabilitation in the School of Health, Community and Education Studies and has recently moved to the University of Edinburgh. He has 30 years' experience working in higher education, initially in a Russell Group university, and then in the post-92 sector. He has maintained an active research profile, contributing to RAE submissions throughout his career. He has developed and managed postgraduate taught and research programmes, supervising to completion 17 Doctorates and five MPhils, and has mentored two PhD by publication students. He was a member of the Impact and Evaluation Group (formerly the Rugby Team) linked to Vitae, who work nationally on the researcher development agenda.

Jennifer Chubb, Research Innovation Officer, University of York, is actively involved in supporting researchers to engage with the Impact Agenda principally through training and development, whilst also advising academic staff on individual grant applications. Jenn joined the University of York from the University of Leeds, where she worked as an Enterprise and Knowledge Transfer Training and Development Officer supporting research students and staff through the development of a wide range of training opportunities across a broad range of disciplines. She has expertise in delivering bespoke and generic courses on research impact, grant writing and knowledge exchange in higher education nationally and internationally. Her background is in philosophy and she is currently pursuing a PhD in the Department of Education at York, examining 'the Impact Agenda and academics' perception of their roles: perspectives from the UK and Australia'.

She is also a Public Engagement Ambassador with the National Co-ordinating Centre for Public Engagement and has delivered impact masterclasses at the University of Western Australia for research students.

Rob Daley is an academic developer with a keen interest in the researcher development agenda. He is currently Director of Researcher Development at the University of York and has previously held academic and researcher development posts at Heriot-Watt University and the University of Leicester. Rob's professional interests and activities cover a wide range of related topics including evaluation of academic development activities, accredited provision for researchers, the role of supervisors in researcher development and issues around research impact.

He is or has been a member of a range of national committees and working groups involved in the researcher development arena. Present membership includes the Vitae Impact and Evaluation Group and the RCUK Schools Policy Advisory Panel for *Chapter Bill: Research Degrees* of the new UK Quality Code and was the QAA Advisory Group. He was a member of the Deputy-chair of the Vitae Research Staff Development Advisory Group. He played a key role in the development of the Vitae Researcher Development Framework and in the development of the 2011 PIRLS survey. Over the last four years Rob has played an active role in Edinburgh Beltane (a beacon for public engagement), supporting researchers at all levels to enhance their public engagement activities.

André de Campos is an economist by training and holds a PhD in Science and Technology Policy Studies at SPRU (University of Sussex). He has held teaching and research posts at the University of Sussex, University of Brighton, Brunel University and Royal Holloway University of London. He is currently a permanent member of staff, teaching economics and management at UNICAMP (University of Campinas – Brazil). His research has been funded by CNPq (Brazil), the European Union and ESRC (United Kingdom). He has also experience in the banking industry and in the public sector, having worked as a placement fellow in the Strategy Unit at Research Councils UK.

Andy Jackson is Head of Business Development at the Higher Education Academy (HEA), where he is responsible for an organisation-wide programme to develop new revenue-generating services and establish an international presence for the HEA and its work. He also delivers training in business development and innovation management to staff and students at universities in the UK and internationally.

Before joining the HEA in October 2010, he was Head of Business Development at the University of York where he led the Research Innovation Office, providing support for the development of translational research across all academic departments. This work involved building and managing interdisciplinary groups and working with a network of public and private sector partners across organisational and international boundaries.

Before joining the University of York, he pursued a successful career in high technology industry, working in technical and then managerial roles with Siemens, Canon and Nokia between 1997 and 2005. He is a Chartered Engineer and registered PRINCE2 practitioner and holds an MBA from the Open University Business School as well as a PhD in Electronics from the University of York, where he undertook research and development work in quantitative Auger electron spectroscopy.

Jo Lakey has a BA (Hons) from Warwick University and was awarded the MBA in Higher Education Management by the Institute of Education, University of London in 2010. She has worked in higher education since 2002 and joined Brunel University in 2007, taking up the post of Research Impact Manager in December 2009. Her role was to devise and implement strategies for the collection of impact data and the effective communication to academic staff about impact. She worked closely with academic staff across the institution to prepare impact case studies for REF2014. Her role included publicising Brunel's impact; for example writing three of the case studies which were included in RCUK's 'Big Ideas for the Future' report (published in June 2011). In September 2012, she moved to the Institute of Education where she project manages REF2014 as part of her role as Research Policy Manager.

Sophie Payne-Gifford is part administrator and part academic. She has seven years of science administration experience at the Research Councils, first in research commissioning at the ESRC on programmes such as the Rural Economy and Land Use programme and is now at NERC as Impact Assessment Portfolio Manager. She develops and manages retrospective evidence of impacts arising from NERC's research for use in strategic communications, particularly those justifying future investment in the science base. Prior to the Comprehensive Spending Review in 2010 she project managed the production of a series of economic valuation reports by the consultancy DTZ. She is currently developing a series of timelines to demonstrate the long timescales from investment to impact as well as qualitative case studies. Sophie's University of Oxford MSc dissertation focused on the Impact Agenda, its development and its implications for future UK research strategy. She is also a part-time PhD student at the University of Reading where she is focusing on the role of regulation in innovation systems.

Ellen Pearce is Director of Vitae and CEO of CRAC, the career development organisation which manages Vitae. She is responsible for the strategy, work and activities of Vitae, which aims to enhance the quality and output of the UK research base, through supporting the training and development of world-class researchers. Working in the area of personal, professional and career development for researchers since 2002, Ellen has been involved in several key initiatives in the last few years. Currently, she is a member of the Impact and Evaluation Group, which is a sector-led working group exploring the effectiveness of skills development for researchers, the NERC Training Advisory Group, the EURAXESS steering group, and the Research Staff Development Advisory Group.

She is a member of the European Commission's Institutional HR Strategy Group to support the implementation of the European Charter and Code for researchers and has led the process for UK institutions to gain the European HR Excellence in Research Award.

She has worked on the 'What do researchers do?' publication series and co-authored 'Enterprise at work: exploring intrapreneurship in researcher development' and 'The visibility of researcher development in UK higher education institutions' strategies'. She has also led work funded by the EC Lifelong Learning programme to enhance doctoral employability through internationally applicable training and development support and university careers services.

Geoff Rodgers gained his BSc in Mathematics at Imperial College and a PhD in theoretical physics at Manchester University. He held a European Postdoctoral Fellowship from the Royal Society at the Service de Physique Théorique, Saclay. Appointed to Brunel University in 1989, he became Pro-Vice-Chancellor for Research in 2008.

The main responsibility of his role is to lead the university in the next stage of its research development, and ensure that it sustains a diverse and evolving, vibrant, research community. He has championed the introduction of an open access archive and publications database as well as developing successful strategic partnerships with a number of research technology organisations. He is a Fellow of the Institute of Physics and the Higher Education Academy. He chairs the Research Excellence Group of London Higher, consisting of the Pro-Vice-Chancellors for Research of the universities in London.

Rosa Scoble graduated from LSE with a degree in Management Sciences and completed a PhD on the RAE2001 at Brunel University before taking up the role of manager of the School of Information Systems, Computing and Mathematics. In 2006 she was appointed director of the university's Research Assessment Exercise 2008 Office.

She is currently Deputy Planning Director (Research and Resources) and as part of her role heads the Research Evaluation Unit. She is now playing a key role in Brunel's preparations for the upcoming Research Excellence Framework, with a particular focus on the Impact Agenda. In 2009 she ran a pilot study that led to the development of BRIDE (Brunel Research Impact Device for Evaluation) based on HERG's Payback Framework.

Her work on impact and the development of BRIDE is captured in a research publication that analyses institutional strategies for capturing and enhancing the socio-economic impact of research.

She has spoken at a number of conferences on how to capture impact in a broad based and multi-disciplinary institution.

Sara Shinton works with universities in the UK and across Europe to create staff and student development programmes with lasting results. A recognised leader in her field, she focuses on giving academic researchers insights into good practice in areas including impact, research funding, collaboration and creativity.

With a background in physical chemistry, careers advice and academic development, she founded Shinton Consulting in 2000 to focus on the development of academic researchers, partly motivated by her own experiences as a postdoctoral researcher. She writes regularly about academic and researcher careers, tackling a diverse range of topics such as building influence, achieving career balance and exploiting social media.

She is passionate about celebrating research and organises a science festival, 'Bang Goes the Borders', which connects families with exciting researchers working at the cutting-edge. See www.shintonconsulting.com for more information.

Christopher Wood is a researcher development manager at the University of Exeter. For many years he was a senior research scientist at the Royal Botanic Gardens, Kew. He has supervised a number of PhD students to completion as well as managing post-doctoral researchers. He still manages to do some research 'on the side' and has worked with colleagues in New Zealand and Australia to enhance orchid and palm conservation. He is an editor of a plant-biology-related international peer review journal.

His passion for developing early career researchers is evident by the many contributions he makes to both regional and national agendas; he was shortlisted for a prestigious Times Higher Education Award for 'excellence in the contribution to researcher development'. He is a Senior Fellow of the Higher Education Academy and sits on the sector-wide 'Impact and Evaluation Group'.

PROLOGUE

HOW AND WHY THIS BOOK CAME INTO BEING

As a contribution to the series Success in Research, edited by Denicolo and Becker, this specific book addresses the topic of impact of research in all its guises, including the impact of researcher development in higher education (HE), as well as issues related to the reporting of achieved impact for the Research Excellence Framework (REF) and of designing potential impact into proposals for research funding.

This book captures the knowledge and experience that the chapter authors and the book editor have gained as researchers and as researcher developers. Several of them, including the editor, have been involved for many years in the Impact and Evaluation Group (previously the Rugby Team – see Appendix I for more information) of Vitae, the UK organisation supported by the Research Councils (RCs) and managed by CRAC, the career development organisation, to champion the personal, professional and career development of doctoral researchers and research staff in higher education and research institutes (see Appendix I for more information).

Some of these and other authors included here contributed to a UK Council for Graduate Education (UKCGE) one-day symposium on the Impact Agenda in Higher Education in Spring 2012. The UKCGE and Vitae are the two leading national organisations concerned with post-graduate education and researcher development respectively. In previous and subsequent conferences of both these and other similarly orientated organisations, the various facets of impact have permeated debates with some passion.

Thus a core team, willing and able to contribute perspectives on the topic, came together and then drew on the further expertise of colleagues in their networks to develop a book that is intended to provide others in higher education with a range of alternative perspectives from which to refine their own ideas and a set of tools with which to engage effectively with the research agenda. As experienced professionals in the field they recognised the need for such a text since the topic frequently appears in policy documents, websites, and during institutional activities but is often ill-defined and poorly understood despite it being especially significant in relation to gaining research funding and the Research Excellence Framework (REF). The latter is the new system for assessing the quality of research in UK higher education institutions (HEIs). Readers from other countries will no doubt be subject to similar quality assessments and requirements to substantiate the worthwhileness of proposed research when seeking funding to support it so will find relevance to their contexts within these chapters.

As in previous books in the series the approach taken in each chapter of this book is to respond to a question that arises in relation to the topic, providing information, activities, reflection points, case studies and advice aimed at researchers, particularly early career researchers, and those who support them. Each author attempts to provide a succinct and accessible source of information distilled from research practice, knowledge and experience, at the same time dispelling any misconceptions that might be held, by new and very experienced academics alike, about the nature of impact and how it can be addressed in relation to research.

Unlike previous books in the series, which are generally jointly or sole authored, this is an edited book with many expert contributors. Nevertheless we have sought to retain a smooth and coherent flow throughout, retaining the different voices but ensuring that any overlap or repetition is included for a specific purpose. For instance, you will find allusion to and discussion of the importance of baseline data in several chapters. This does not make for redundancy but rather illustrates both its importance for judging impact and the various ways that it might be considered and achieved. Similarly different authors discuss the issue of blue sky research, bringing different aspects to light and providing a range of perspectives. More than one chapter refers to the Researcher Development Framework (RDF) so a summary diagram that presents its key features is included as Appendix II. Similarly the Research Councils UK diagram 'Pathways to Impact' is mentioned in more than one chapter so this appears as Appendix III. Each author is adding a tile to the mosaic of understanding of the Impact Agenda and how it can be fruitfully enacted. Throughout the book there will be forward and backward referencing and sign-posting to aid the reader in navigating the text; the team also agreed a comprehensive glossary of commonly used, but not necessarily commonly understood, words and phrases related to research impact and an index to assist readers to find other examples and references to topics to compare their nuances.

It is important to note here that there has been considerable debate in the sector about the notion of impact as applied to research. Proponents have ranged from those considering that it is simply another way of expressing the desire that all researchers have always had to conduct research that is not trivial and has results of some consequence, to those who see the Impact Agenda as an external, politico-economic imposition on research in higher education which not only ignores the value of 'blue-skies' or research on topics simply because they are interesting but also diverts research effort into areas that produce fast, identifiable impact that 'counts' in audit exercises. This controversy is not ignored in the book but given consideration in various ways so that the readers can form their own perspectives. In particular, the issue is raised and explored by Colin Chandler in Chapter 1, addressed by Sophie Payne-Gifford in Chapter 2 while Jennifer Chubb reports the views of academic participants in her research in Chapter 3. How the story of research impact is played out in academia is elaborated throughout the book, as can be seen from the chapter summaries below.

SUMMARY OF CHAPTERS

Chapter 1: in this chapter Colin Chandler addresses the question, 'What is the meaning of impact in relation to research and why does it matter? A view from inside academia'. He provides some definitions of impact with a historical overview of how these concepts emerged within the academy, which then forms the background to his analysis of recent debate, including the challenges that it presents, and the current picture of the Impact Agenda as apparently driving research directions. He suggests that the ways in which we understand or define impact help us to determine the significance and reach of research.

Chapter 2: this chapter, entitled 'What is the meaning of the Impact Agenda – is it a repackaged or a new entity? Views from inside the Research Councils' by Sophie Payne-Gifford, considers the notion that the Impact Agenda is merely a construction of an old idea into a new format by examining the evidence for and against this proposition. Evidence supporting the proposition takes a historical view of impact being a reformulation of the original mission of the Research Councils as set out in the

Royal Charters, namely to conduct research for the good of the UK economy. However, as she takes a closer look at the inner workings of the Research Councils, there is enough evidence to suggest that something has indeed changed. The chapter reconciles these two opposing opinions by drawing on the philosophical views of critical realists that allow both statements to be true at the same time. It also draws on the author's Master's dissertation as well as her professional experience within the Research Councils.

In Chapter 3 Jennifer Chubb builds on the concepts raised in Chapters 1 and 2 by demonstrating the empirical findings of a qualitative study around academic attitudes to impact in order to address the question, 'How does the Impact Agenda fit with attitudes and ethics that motivate research?' She outlines the differing motives for carrying out research and the perceptions offered by different disciplines on the challenges posed by the Impact Agenda. She addresses the problem of making sense of the agenda in a way that does not compromise integrity or the motivation for doing research in the first place. She hopes that her research results will reassure, motivate and engage others in dealing with the Impact Agenda.

In Chapter 4, Jo Lakey, Geoff Rodgers and Rosa Scoble join forces to address the question, 'What are the different characteristics of research impact?' As they address issues such as the time taken for impact to emerge, how different disciplines generate and characterise impact and the different types of impact that can emerge, they seek to help researchers understand the impact routes that their own and other different disciplines might follow and the types of research this would encompass.

Chapter 5 addresses Christopher Wood's question 'When might research impact be apparent?' as he concentrates on when we would expect to see the impacts of research and what can influence this timing. He also considers the differences that having baseline data can make and what may lead to a delay in making impact assessments. Finally consideration is given to when we would expect to see the impact of developing our researchers.

In Chapter 6, Rob Daley and Sara Shinton address the question, 'How can impact be planned into research proposals?' They provide guidance to researchers who are writing funding bids on including elements of impact within their research proposals. The different considerations required of a researcher at various stages of the proposal development are explained along with some key tips and a checklist of the most important aspects and inclusions. Consideration is given to how referees view impact and the cost of impact-related activity so that readers can prepare well their future proposals, drawing on examples from a number of case studies from a cross-section of disciplines and including collaborative projects.

In Chapter 7 the question 'How can impact evaluation be planned?' is addressed by Tony Bromley and André de Campos, who provide a methodology for evaluating impact. They outline the theoretical basis for the evaluation methodology and discuss: the planning of impact evaluation; the strategic choice of an 'object' of study; and the use of logic diagrams in the evaluation and reflection on the results of an evaluation. As they do so, they offer practical insights for the management of an impact study, for example covering the organisation of tasks into work packages, study implementation and risk issues.

In Chapter 8 Tony Bromley addresses the question 'How can impact be evidenced: practical methods?' Building on the concepts raised in Chapter 7 he considers methods of collecting data as part of a robust evaluation. Using examples from his current work practice, he provides details of some key methods used in evaluation, and addresses their limitations, the common pitfalls and considerations to be addressed in choosing the correct method that will provide the data required for a given evaluation.

We meet Jennifer Chubb again in Chapter 9 as she tackles the question, 'What skills are needed to be an impactful researcher?' In this very interactive chapter she discusses the skills necessary to engage with a range of audiences, considering who, why and in what ways they might be interested, as she guides us through the RCUK Pathways to Impact document.

Chapter 10 finds Andy Jackson reflecting on the question, 'How can knowledge exchange support the development of impact through partnerships and university infrastructures?' In this chapter, having clarified the concept of knowledge exchange, he discusses, among other things, marketing the benefits of research to non-academic audiences, and identifying and engaging in partnerships and support services both internal and external.

In Chapter 11, Ellen Pearce and Pam Denicolo use the stimulus of the question 'How can you become an impactful researcher?' to summarise the key messages contained in the book as an impetus to readers to continue to develop their own skills in addressing the Impact Agenda to suit individual circumstances. A case study of research with impact is provided to whet the appetite of those contemplating new research projects.

HOW YOU MIGHT USE THIS BOOK

Although we have tried to work through the topic of impact in research in a logical order that provides a flow of ideas, there is no need, unless it suits your learning style and current knowledge about the topic, to start at the beginning and work chapter by chapter to the end. Instead, you may choose to read the chapters in the order that addresses the questions that arise for you in your situation. At the beginning of each chapter you will find a summary in bullet point form of the key content areas, so you might like first to read each of these to help guide your route through parts of the book that will be of most use to you. Contributors have each provided their own Reference list at the end of their chapter and some have provided a list of Resources that you might find useful. Further, we have attempted to alert you within each chapter to links to other chapters, for instance where a topic is covered in more depth or from a different perspective elsewhere, so you might follow theme threads as they emerge.

An important point is that this book is not intended to simply provide information, useful though that might be for you. We also seek to engage you actively both in considering issues to develop your own arguments and in developing skills of building impact into your research and demonstrating it effectively. Thus the chapter authors have provided activities and exercises to help you with this aim and added to their contribution signposts to other work that might extend or elaborate on what they have provided in a short chapter. In addition, some have illustrated their ideas with case studies so that you can gain an insight into how these ideas might appear in practice.

As with all emergent perspectives in any realm of human activity, a new vocabulary has evolved alongside the Impact Agenda, which consists of individual words, names of processes and so on, and acronyms. We have attempted to introduce newcomers to the topic by providing a Glossary at the end of the book that gives some guidance on the current meaning of this vocabulary.

1

WHAT IS THE MEANING OF IMPACT IN RELATION TO RESEARCH AND WHY DOES IT MATTER? A VIEW FROM INSIDE ACADEMIA

COLIN CHANDLER

Key points

- Definitions of impact
- The changing academic viewpoint on impact
- Some challenges confronted
- The emerging picture of impact

Impact is a commonly used term but in the research context it is gaining more importance. It is most often assumed that the meaning of impact is clearly understood and interpreted in the same way by researchers, funding bodies, policy-makers and the public, but we might consider whether this is the case.

REFLECTION POINT

Before you read any further you might want to jot down what you understand by impact in the context of research so that you can compare it to the definitions provided here.

Impact in its simplest definition is about making a difference, so there is action or activity which leads to change, but that change needs to be seen within a context which may be global, local or even individual. Also the nature of the change needs to be considered, whether it is related to people, systems, environment, knowledge, understanding or policy.

So this simple definition of impact, *making a difference*, needs to be developed to be useful to researchers and research funders. Researchers are now being asked to look back at their research and identify the impact it has had as well as to look forward and predict what impact their ongoing and future research will have. These issues have historically been implicit, assumed within the research ethos of the academic community, but are now being required as explicit statements to justify and secure ongoing and future funding from public, private or charitable funds.

This chapter will:

- explore these definitions of impact further;
- look at the change in approach to impact over the last decade and the debates around this change from an academic viewpoint;
- draw together the emerging picture of impact as an element driving research direction in the twenty-first century to set the scene for the later chapters of this book.

Exploring definitions

There are many definitions of impact circulating at present; I am taking three which broadly cover the range. The Arts and Humanities Research Council (AHRC) has shown considerable interest in establishing impact within their remit and say, 'By impact we mean the "influence" of research or its "effect on" an individual, a community, the development of policy, or the creation of a new product or service. It relates to the effects of research on our economic, social and cultural lives' (AHRC, 2010: 1); the Research Councils UK (RCUK) emphasise the link with excellence in their definition: 'Impact is the demonstrable contribution that excellent research makes to society and the economy' (RCUK, 2011: 2); and the Research Excellence Framework 'REF2014' defines impact as '… an effect on, change or benefit to the economy, society, culture, public policy or services, health, the environment or quality of life, beyond academia' (REF, 2011: 48). These definitions combined show that impact is far wider than just knowledge creation within academia.

These definitions enable us to look at the nature of impact, the relevance of context and the outcomes or indicators of impact. The nature of impact is identified as the influence, effect, demonstrable contribution, change or benefits that result from the research. The context within which that impact takes place is broad beyond academia in the realms of society, economy, public policy or services, health, the environment or quality of life. The outcomes or indicators of impact encompass the individual, community or global levels and are the application of new knowledge or understanding in the development of policy, creation of products or services. Impact is largely considered from an anthropocentric viewpoint but effects on non-human subjects and environment need to be considered as well. Impact is also implicitly of benefit to society drawing on the ethical principles of causing no harm (non-maleficence) and doing good (beneficence) within an essentially utilitarian concept, namely the greatest good for the greatest number.

A changing academic viewpoint

The emerging picture of impact is driving research direction in the twenty-first century. This paradigm shift, a change in the way we are viewing research in higher education, is both changing practice among researchers and changing the behaviours of research funders. As with many changes, this has led to much debate and controversy within the sector; however, to use the words of the Research Councils, it is seeking demonstrable 'Excellence with impact' (RCUK, 2007). (More information about the Research Councils' perspectives can be found in the next chapter.) This focus on impact could be seen to have parallels with research training, which was brought to the fore in the Roberts review 'Set for success' in 2002 (Roberts, 2002) where the need for a wider training was identified in doctoral education to better fit researchers to the needs of industry and subsequently society in general. The powerhouse of postgraduate research must not be underestimated as the pipeline to the development of highly skilled individuals who will not only populate higher education in the future but also be key drivers and leaders in the social, economic and cultural development of healthy societies in the UK and across the world. In this time of global reach in our universities we must also consider the global impact of our and our students' activities.

Thomas Kuhn, in his analysis of the history of science, used the term *paradigm shift* to explain the step changes in worldview that occurred following a new discovery, or way of thinking (Kuhn, 1996). Over the past decade, the worldview of the nature and purpose of research has changed with respect to the issue of impact.

This is exemplified by a number of specific changes (see Box 1.1) which are addressed below:

BOX 1.1   CHANGES IN THE WAY RESEARCH IS VIEWED

From	To
Implicit	Explicit
Research – an end in its own right	Focused and forward-looking research
Curiosity driven	Targeted
Academic freedom	Constrained
Self-regulated	Governance
Serendipity	Investment
Academic excellence	Excellence with impact

Within the research community there has been an implicit understanding that research makes a difference – it may not be immediate, but the growth of knowledge about our world and about our ways in society would inevitably contribute to its development. The evidence of the nineteenth century with its rapid technical and industrial development speaks for itself. The technological developments in the second half of the last century have changed the way we work, communicate and live. Much of this development has been led through university research.

Over this period there was a massive expansion of the university sector in the 1960s with the building of new universities and the establishment of the polytechnics and then in the 1990s with the inclusion of the former polytechnics into the university sector. Throughout this period, university education expanded from the province of the select few, to the experience of a substantial proportion of young people and an increasing number of mature students. Alongside this, the postgraduate and academic opportunities also expanded to service the growing university population. Research was an implicit part of the university academic's work and its impact was passed on through teaching and academic publication in the main part.

Over the past decade, there has been an increasing demand to make explicit the purpose of each research endeavour and the difference or impact it will make or has made. As *The Times* headline in 2010 stated, 'Prove the benefits of research or lose funds' (Hurst and Henderson, 2010), and as a senior member of the funding council is reported to have said when defending the inclusion of impact in the next assessment exercise – REF2014, 'Showing the impact of research beyond University walls makes good political sense' (Lane, 2011).

When the requirement to show how research may make an impact was introduced, considerable argument was made around academic freedom and the need for research as an end in its own right where the impact would be seen in retrospect in the longer term. This was based on the argument that at the time that the research was undertaken, the difference that it would make (if any) to future society was unknown. Examples were cited of Newton's definition of the laws of motion, which underpin the majority of engineering applications today, and the discovery of radium and polonium by Marie Curie with the development of the theory of radioactivity, which have led to advances in many diverse fields, for example medicine and weapons development. In contrast, the shift has led to more focused and forward-looking research where pressure has led to thought and argument being put into some prediction of the potential of the research for the future. This is often speculative in nature but has led to a more future oriented, focused and forward looking approach. Perhaps this can be seen as making explicit the implicit expectations, hopes and dreams of researchers.

Confronting some challenges

Is there then a threat to curiosity-driven research? Perhaps, and fears were certainly expressed over the narrow perception of impact, that it was being focused mainly on economics, that followed the publication of the Warry Report (Warry, 2006). However subsequent work, in particular in the area of the arts and humanities, has helped develop a wider understanding of impact in broader societal terms (AHRC, 2008). Targeting research into potential benefit areas does not necessarily prevent curiosity-driven research, but does require researchers to consider the trajectory and potential benefit of their research, which in turn can address the current Impact Agenda. This has been clearly demonstrated in the arts and humanities areas, which may have felt most threatened, through the AHRC case studies and the Rand study based at Cambridge University (AHRC, 2008; Levitt et al., 2010).

Perhaps the loudest *cri de coeur* has arisen over the perceived erosion of academic freedom. Academic freedom is perhaps already an illusion which has been constrained now for years through funding mechanisms and the need to convince funders that a research idea is worth funding and within their remit. Hence constraint has existed previously, but the question still remains about whether impact is now adding a further strand to that constraint. Underlying the above points is perhaps the fundamental concern that blue-skies, curiosity-driven research, will be replaced by applied research only focused on short-term goals with clear and obvious return.

This concern is perhaps upheld when consideration is given to modes of funding where an increasing volume of commissioned research is being funded compared to response mode funding. The Research Councils, though, continue to base their research project funding primarily on response mode. However EU funding is predominantly commissioned and charities are mixed but constrained by their charitable purposes. Private sector funding tends to be contract based with a clear view to a return on their investment.

Another shift has been the increasing development of the governance and public accountability agendas to replace self-regulation, or at least peer regulation, within the academic community. Transparency over the use of resources in higher education for teaching and research has been explored through TRAC returns (Transparent Approach to Costing) (HEFCE, 2009). It is clear that public, voluntary sector and private funders all want to see a return on the investments they make. However the opportunities presented with the current Impact Agenda are for the universities to demonstrate the breadth and diversity of that impact. In the Knowledge Exchange arena much play is made over the creation of KTPs (knowledge transfer partnerships) and spin-out companies, though this ignores the majority of the impact of knowledge exchange which occurs through informal contacts between universities and organisations often through the medium of postgraduate education. It is no surprise when employers comment on postgraduate provision: *'These programmes not only changed people's lives but led to genuine improvements in policy and practice'* (Northumbria University, 2007).

The governance agenda has also led to the creation of many opportunities within universities for posts encompassing the Impact agenda and has undoubtedly led to an increase in the administrative burden on researchers and university managers. However, this parallels the increasing need for public accountability across all areas of the public sector.

The emerging picture of impact

Whether by good luck or good planning, we have moved from a situation where impact is the serendipitous outcome of research, to one where the investment of funders needs to be seen. A number of reports over the last decade have led to the need to demonstrate in particular with our students the skills outcomes of research training. The Roberts review, 'Set for Success' (Roberts, 2002), initiated the postgraduate skills agenda and has, through the resultant funding streams, led to the development of a wider skills training and now on to the Researcher Development Framework (see Appendices I and II), extending this concept to the researcher's lifelong career (Vitae, 2011). Support mechanisms focused on researcher development ensure that doctoral candidates, and to some growing extent postdoctoral researchers, have access to training and other opportunities to expand their skill set. The emphasis is on the wider skills that feed into impact-like activities. The Leitch and Warry reports (Leitch, 2006; Warry, 2006) followed this up, further supporting the need to develop wider researcher skills. Alongside this has come the question of what return the funders are getting on their investment. Vitae, through the Impact and Evaluation Group (see Appendix I) developed a tool – the five-stage impact framework (Bromley and Metcalfe, 2012) to address this challenging question. The highest level of this looks at the long-term benefits of the training and is certainly the most difficult to quantify. Demonstration of this level of impact is reliant on case examples where, of course, a myriad of other factors and experience may contribute. This reflects the complex reality of the researcher's context.

There is no doubt about the legacy of the academic excellence of research over the past decades, though the shift needs to be, in the words of the Research Councils, to excellence with impact (RCUK, 2007). This paradigm shift is on-going. The research landscape is complex and, as the recent REF impact pilot demonstrated, there is still much learning to be achieved for the sector to demonstrate this aspect effectively (REF2014, 2010). The complexity of the research contexts must not be underestimated and different disciplines must be allowed to respond in their own way to reflect the real world impacts that they demonstrate in their own specific contexts.

The features of the paradigm shift described above are more embedded in newer researchers as exemplified by recent doctoral graduates. The doctoral degree in the UK is essentially a research degree in which the student engages in original research and makes an original contribution to knowledge (QAA, 2011). In professional doctorates this contribution is linked in some way to the professional perspective through theoretical or practical development (QAA, 2011). It is interesting to note that these contributions do not specifically have to demonstrate impact. This diversity of programmes reflects the range of doctoral research. They include major discovery or establishing new theory (but these are rare), although more commonly moving knowledge forward through the use of novel methodology, a new application of existing techniques or knowledge applied in a new context. The analogy of a wall can be useful here, where the modest contribution of the doctorate can be described as adding another brick in the wall of knowledge. However, the change in emphasis in doctoral education with concurrent researcher development training has led to researchers who are better equipped to communicate and engage with the public over the impact of their research. Perhaps we could say that they are not just producing a brick but ensuring that it is carefully set in the wall!

This can be illustrated by an encounter I had with a professor in the middle of an Indian city where western medicine rubbed shoulders with abject poverty. He said, 'the important thing is that we make a difference in individuals' lives.' An example from my own area of research is where an appropriate intervention supported by telemedicine saved the life of a Nepali lady. This has led to recognition of important principles which have been explored more widely in Nepal and are now informing telemedicine development in other areas of the world (Lama et al., 2011). Working with an individual and specific focus remains important, but retaining the wider view of where the research is going and what effect it may have embraces the Impact Agenda.

So I suggest our emerging understandings of impact should embrace a range of definitions, shown in Box 1.2.

BOX 1.2   A COLLATION OF HELPFUL DEFINITIONS OF IMPACT

To have impact is to have a strong effect, to make a difference.

By impact we mean the 'influence' of research or its 'effect on' an individual, a community, the development of policy, or the creation of a new product or service. It relates to the effects of research on our economic, social and cultural lives (AHRC, 2010).

Impact is the demonstrable contribution that excellent research makes to society and the economy (RCUK, 2011).

Impact … an effect on, change or benefit to the economy, society, culture, public policy or services, health, the environment or quality of life, beyond academia (REF, 2011).

These suggest that we must consider the nature of research impact, the context of research impact and the outcome or effect of research impact. These features will help us to recognise the *significance* or importance of the research and its *reach* or pervasiveness into society.

References

AHRC (2008) 'At home in Renaissance Italy – an impact case study'. Available at: http://media.vam.ac.uk/media/documents/legacy_documents/file_upload/44451_file.pdf

AHRC (2010) 'Impact Summary and Pathways to Impact Frequently Asked Questions – AHRC'. Available at: http://www.ahrc.ac.uk/Funding-Opportunities/Documents/ImpactFAQ.pdf (accessed 30 September 2012).

Bromley, T. and Metcalfe, J. (2012) 'The impact framework 2012'. Available at: http://www.vitae.ac.uk/impact

HEFCE (2009) 'Policy overview of the financial management information needs of higher education, and the role of TRAC'. Available at: http://www.hefce.ac.uk/media/hefce/content/whatwedo/leadershipgovernanceandmanagement/financialsustainabilityandtrac/tracforseniormanagers/policy-overview-2009.pdf.

Hurst, G. and Henderson, M. (2010) 'Prove the benefits of research or lose funds', *The Times* (London), 12 November: 30, 31.

Kuhn, T.S. (1996) *The Structure of Scientific Revolutions*, 3rd edition, Chicago: University of Chicago Press.

Lama, T., Karmachary, B., Chandler, C. and Patterson, V., 2011) 'Telephone management of severe wasp stings in rural Nepal: a case report', *Journal of Telemedicine and Telecare*, 17(2): 105–8. Available at: http://www.ncbi.nlm.nih.gov/pubmed/21139015 (accessed 1 October 2012).

Lane, B. (2011) 'Let others judge research impact', *The Australian*, 2 November: 21.

Leitch, S. (2006) 'Prosperity for all in the global economy – world class skills', Available at: http://www.hm-treasury.gov.uk/d/leitch_finalreport051206.pdf.

Levitt, R., Celia, C., Diepeveen, S., Ní Chonaill, S., Rabinovich, L. and Tiessen, J. (2010) *Assessing the Impact of Arts and Humanities Research at the University of Cambridge*. A RAND Corporation Report prepared for the University of Cambridge and the Arts and Humanities Research Council. Available at: http://www.rand.org/content/dam/rand/pubs/technical_reports/2010/RAND_TR816.pdf (accessed 1 October 2012). Northumbria University (2007) Periodic review report: PG Multi Disciplinary Programmes. Available at: http://www.northumbria.ac.uk/static/worddocuments/ardocs/pgmdp2007.doc (accessed 30 September 2012).

QAA (2011) 'The UK doctorate: a guide for current and prospective doctoral candidates'. Available at: http://www.qaa.ac.uk/Publications/InformationAndGuidance/Documents/Doctorate_Guide.pdf

RCUK (2007) 'Excellence with impact'. Available at: http://www.rcuk.ac.uk/documents/economicimpact/excellenceimpact.pdf

RCUK (2011) 'RCUK impact requirements frequently asked questions'. Available at: http://www.rcuk.ac.uk/documents/impacts/RCUKImpactFAQ.pdf (accessed 30 September 2012).

REF (2011) 'REF2014: assessment framework and guidance on submissions REF 02.2012'. Available at: http://www.ref.ac.uk/media/ref/content/pub/assessmentframeworkandguidanceonsubmissions/02_11.pdf.

REF2014 (2010) 'Research excellence framework impact pilot exercise: findings of the expert panels (November)'. Available at: http://www.ref.ac.uk/pubs/refimpactpilotexercisefindingsoftheexpertpanels/ (accessed 1 October 2012).

Roberts, G. (2002) *SET for Success*, London: HM Treasury, public.enquiries@hm-treasury.gsi.gov.uk. Available at: http://webarchive.nationalarchives.gov.uk/+/http://www.hm-treasury.gov.uk/set_for_success.htm (accessed 30 September 2012).

Vitae (2011) 'Researcher development framework'. Available at: http://www.vitae.ac.uk/rdf

Warry, P. (2006) 'Increasing the economic impact of Research Councils'. Available at: http://www.vitae.ac.uk/policy-practice/201891/Warry-Report.html

2

WHAT IS THE MEANING OF THE IMPACT AGENDA – IS IT A REPACKAGED OR A NEW ENTITY? VIEWS FROM INSIDE THE RESEARCH COUNCILS

SOPHIE PAYNE-GIFFORD[1]

Key points

- Opinions on the Impact Agenda vary
- The focus on impact has a history going back decades
- The Research Councils are undergoing a number of changes implementing the Impact Agenda

Introduction

In the midst of consultation and controversy about impact and research, one opinion presented is that there is no 'Impact Agenda', that it is a

---

[1]The author is and has been an employee of the Research Councils since 2005 and has been employed at the Natural Environment Research Council since 2009 in the role of Impact Assessment Portfolio Manager. The reader may choose to see this as a source of bias or as a source of insight. This chapter is not an official Research Council position.

construction.[2] For those readers unfamiliar with social theory, 'a construction' occurs when 'the phenomenon in question [is] a product of our particular society or societies like it, rather than being something which is natural or inevitable' (Crossley, 2005). In the case of the Impact Agenda, to suggest it is a construction suggests that it is a creation of our collective imaginations. In other words, the focus on impact is nothing new; it is only that now we are making a big song and dance about it. You may wonder, then, if there is no actual 'Impact Agenda', why does this book or chapter exist? As there is resistance to and misunderstandings about the changes in the UK's science system, it is useful to confront this controversy. This allows you, the reader, to develop your own opinions, and may help you to understand some of the conversations you may hear your more senior colleagues engaged in.

This chapter contributes to this book by considering whether the Impact Agenda *is* a construction by examining evidence for and against this proposition using the Research Councils as a case study. Evidence supporting the proposition takes a historical view of impact being a reformulation of the original mission of the Research Councils, namely to conduct research for the good of the UK. However, if we take a closer look at the inside workings of the Research Councils, there is enough evidence to suggest that something tangible has changed. I reconcile these two apparently opposing opinions by drawing on philosophical views that allow both statements to be true at the same time. This chapter draws on my 2009 Master's dissertation on the Impact Agenda as well as my professional experience within the Research Councils. Of course, this chapter only tells half the story of the Impact Agenda as it does not discuss the role of the higher education funding councils and the Research Excellence Framework (the REF) due to lack of space, but other chapters in the book will mention these perspectives.

Evidence against an Impact Agenda

The current focus

Let us start with the current focus on impact. The 2006 Warry Report *Increasing the Economic Impact of Research Councils*, which you will see mentioned

---

[2]This opinion was received as anonymous referee feedback on an unsuccessful journal submission: 'the very idea of an "impact agenda" is a construction' (anonymous personal correspondence). It is this comment that has inspired this chapter.

a few times in this book, is often credited as the source of the current focus, including my interviewees. This report called on the Research Councils to pursue a number of issues including knowledge transfer and user engagement (see Box 2.1).

BOX 2.1   EXCERPT FROM THE WARRY REPORT

Three key issues on which the Research Councils must act:

- their **leadership** of the knowledge transfer agenda;
- their role in **influencing** knowledge transfer behaviour of universities and Research Council Institutes;
- increasing their **engagement** with user organisations. (Warry, 2006: 2, bold in original)

One of the responses to the Warry Report (and there are others) was the inclusion of an 'impact plan' with all new grant applications from 2009. In it applicants were asked to consider the potential impacts their research may have and the routes to making this impact more likely with funds available for relevant impact-making activities. To clarify the purpose of an impact plan (and to respond to criticisms from the academic community) the Research Councils renamed this document 'Pathways to Impact': '[W]e believe that the name was obscuring the purpose, which is for researchers to explore Pathways to Impact, not to accurately predict the impacts of work yet to be undertaken' (RCUK, no date). See Chapter 6 for more information on how to plan routes for impact into your own research.

Looking a bit further backwards, the *2004–2014 Science and Innovation Investment Framework* published by the Treasury (HM Treasury, 2004) was also identified by interviewees in my research project as an earlier precursor to the Impact Agenda (see Box 2.2 for excerpt). It obliged the Research Councils to agree goals for knowledge transfer rates and foreshadowed the introduction of the REF. The *Framework* set up a 10-year reporting framework so that Research Council performance could be monitored, and so that the science base's contribution to the UK's economy could be tracked through the keeping of metrics (more on this in the next section).

BOX 2.2   EXCERPT FROM 2004–2014 FRAMEWORK ON AMBITIONS FOR UK SCIENCE AND INNOVATION

Greater responsiveness of the publicly funded research base to the needs of the *economy* and *public services*:

- Research Councils' programmes to be more strongly influenced by and delivered in partnership with *end users* of research
- Continue to improve UK performance in knowledge transfer and commercialisation from universities and public labs towards world leading benchmarks. (HM Treasury, 2004: 6, italics added for emphasis)

Pre-2000s

Other interviewees (with longer memories than my own) traced the Impact Agenda further back than either the Warry Report or the 2004–2014 Framework. Specifically, a few interviewees traced it back to the 1993 Science White Paper *Realising our Potential* (HMSO, 1993), which was credited with an increased focus on knowledge transfer at the Research Councils:

> The story goes back many years, to the 93/94 Science White Paper. An MP produced a paper about the UK funding science at similar level to Japan but that we didn't exploit results with the same effect. As a result, the Research Councils changed their missions, restructured [themselves]. (Senior Research Council interviewee, July 2009)

It was around this time that the Engineering and Physical Sciences Research Council (EPSRC) introduced a statement on the importance of beneficiaries. Another Research Council employee identified this as a step 'en route to pathways to impact' (anonymous correspondence, December 2012). Interestingly, the current criticisms of the Impact Agenda bear similarities to the criticisms of the Reaching Our Potential Awards scheme of 1994–5 (see for example, Motluk, 1995).

Even further back

Employees of various Research Councils advised me to look at the Royal Seals on display in Swindon (see Box 2.3 for excerpt). In linking the Impact

Agenda to the Royal Charter, the interviewees were implicitly tracing it back as far at the 1965 Science and Technology Act setting up the Research Councils.[3] The original text of the Science and Technology Act did not at the time use the words 'impact', 'users' or 'economic competitiveness' but did state that the Research Councils were bodies for 'the dissemination of knowledge[4].'

BOX 2.3   SUMMARY OF ROYAL CHARTERS

Put briefly, the purposes of the Research Councils are to:

1. fund high quality research;
2. advance knowledge and technology to meet the needs of users;
3. contribute to UK economic competitiveness.

(based on Section 2 of current Royal Charter text)
To read the full text of the Royal Charters you do not need to travel all the way to Swindon. Many of them are available online.

The idea that publicly funded science should benefit the UK was formalised in 1965 long before the phrase 'economic impact' was circulating in the worlds of academia or administration. The idea was reincarnated in the 1993 Science White Paper, the 2004–2014 Framework, the Warry Report and finally in its implementation at the Research Councils.

REFLECTION POINT 〜〜

Does your own experience of the Impact Agenda confirm or reject the idea that it really is not anything new?

Evidence for a new Impact Agenda

The above historical analysis might suggest that we can confidently assert that there is no new Impact Agenda. Another view from within the Research Councils may suggest otherwise.

---

[3]The specific Research Councils established in 1965 were the Science Research Council (now EPSRC and STFC) and the Natural Environment Research Council. The Medical Research Council, however, traces its history back as far as 1913.
[4]Science and Technology Act, §1, para. 2 and para. 3.

Consultant reports

One of the first responses to the Warry Report was a flurry of consultant–produced reports considering how the Research Councils might measure the impact of their research and use case studies to illustrate the proposed methodology. For example, PA Consulting Group and SQW were commissioned to produce *Study on the Economic Impact of the Research Councils*, which includes a collection of 18 case studies from across the seven funders (RCUK et al., 2007). Its executive summary states that the report was meant to establish a baseline against which future progress could be measured as well as to demonstrate the different types of impact that research may have.

The purpose of this, and other consultant-led exercises (e.g. PWC, 2006 for NERC), is two-fold, with one purpose explicit and one implicit. The overt purpose is methodological, to consider how impact should or could be evaluated, measured, valued. The implicit purpose of these documents is that they are also advocacy documents. One of my interviewees was critical of one of these consultant reports saying, 'They don't do more than tell nice stories' (Research Council interviewee, July 2009).

However, telling the nice stories is a partial success in itself. It demonstrates that tax-payers' money has been used appropriately and that impact has been occurring without a formal impact framework being in place. It demonstrates to the tax-payer that scientists are not necessarily navel-gazing in their ivory towers (or whatever it is thought that academics do by those with little personal contact with them).

Diagramming

One of the (by)products of these consulting exercises is a number of diagrams explaining routes to impact (see Figure 2.1).

These diagrams (there are others) identify for potential applicants various routes to impact and illustrate that Research Councils are not expecting researchers to change the type of research they conduct (more on this in Chapters 3 and 4). These diagrams also explain to Research Council staff, external peer reviewers, and (not insignificantly) to the parent body of the Research Councils, the Department for Business Innovation and Skills (BIS), the different ways their research communities contribute to social and economic wellbeing of the UK.

Reporting

As mentioned previously, one of the results of the 2004–2014 Framework was to set up a system of reporting on metrics for the 10-year period so

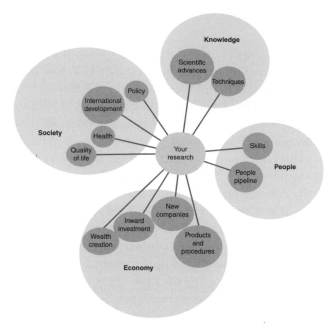

FIGURE 2.1 EPSRC diagram of types and routes to impact (EPSRC, no date)

that progress against key performance indicators could be tracked. For example, in the 2005–06 Outputs Framework, the Economic and Social Research Council (ESRC) reported to the Department for Business Innovation and Skills (BIS) the following: the number of studentships awarded (740), the number of publications arising from ESRC awards (4,695), the number of collaborative projects (82) and about 69 other key performance indicators (ESRC, 2006). There is some narrative in these documents but its focus is on output metrics. The implementation of the Impact Agenda appeared part-way through this 10-year cycle so, wanting to preserve the method of data collection and presentation, the collection of these performance indicators was not redesigned. Now, each Research Council publishes an Impact Report (e.g. NERC, 2011) with metrics *and* case studies and supporting narrative on how it contributes to the health, wellbeing, economy and competitiveness of the UK.

The application process

The Warry Report also encouraged the academic community to take note of impact 'in the terms under which funding is awarded' (Warry, 2006), which resulted in the inclusion of impact in the Research Council funding application process. Many of the researchers I interviewed felt that it was useful to make applicants think about impact, and Pathways to Impact does that. And I believe this plan becomes more than a superficial box-ticking exercise: the post-Foucauldian literature on power and governing tells us that an array of techniques is used to govern, including statistics, census, mapping, and collecting data in general (Rose, 1996). This may be what Rose has in mind when he argues that the governing of individual behaviour arises from writing things down (Rose, 1996). So it is more than useful, because the simple act of putting one's attention on some-thing, of simply thinking about it, changes behaviour; therefore writing a plan of potential routes to impact subtly (or not so subtly) commits the researcher to trying to make it happen.

Organisational structure

Organisational changes within the Natural Environment Research Council (NERC) also suggest the Impact Agenda is more than just a construction. My own experience supports this contention: I was initially recruited into NERC in 2009 on a one-year contract to project-manage a series of consultant-produced impact reports. These were much like the reports discussed above in that they attempted to assess the value of impacts arising from NERC's research.[5] Before the year had ended, my contract had been converted to a permanent, open-ended one. A shorter term need (resulting from a maternity vacancy) had turned into a longer term need for a person to continue developing impact evidence long after the colleague had returned from her leave. Not only that, my actual day-to-day activities have broadened; I am now responsible for delivering a variety of analyses as well as co-ordination of a portfolio of impact evidence activities.

   More recently, NERC's central office has been restructured, creating an Innovation and Communication Directorate so that we co-ordinate the stories of past impact more effectively and also so that we ensure the increase of future impact. An Impact Evidence Team (of which I am part) has been established in this new directorate, whereas before the collection and development of impact stories was dispersed over several business units including Corporate Reporting and Strategy, Knowledge Exchange, and Communications. We are also developing a more organised plan for communicating successes and impacts to our parent department, as well as to the media and other government departments. We have also created a

---

[5]All reports available at www.nerc.ac.uk/business/casestudies/reports.asp

business engagement plan to increase NERC's interactions with the private sector.[6]

REFLECTION POINT 〰

Does the consulting, diagramming, reporting seem like window-dressing to you? Or does it seem like more? If your organisation were engaged in these activities would you feel that actual commitment exists?

In my opinion, even if the term 'Impact Agenda' was a construction when it first entered public discussion, namely an idea formed from the collective imaginations of the UK research system, its administrative implementation is giving it life and a stable reality.

Reconciliation/conclusion

Who is right? As an employee of the Research Councils I must surely see the drivers of my job function as more than a mere 'construction'. If we take the well-known story of the blind men and the elephant, all are accurately describing the elephant from a particular perspective. The notion that different experiences of the same phenomenon are possible and valid also has a basis in modern social theory in the philosophising of the critical realists (e.g. Archer et al., 1998). These philosophers argue that there is a stable reality but that our observation and experience of this reality is only ever partial. This then makes it possible for an academic based in a UK university to feel that not much has changed under the Impact Agenda whereas an employee of the Research Councils can feel the transformation of the Research Councils (and indeed the UK research base) has occured. Philosophically, both are true experiences of the external reality of the 'Impact Agenda' shaped by our differing personal and professional experiences.

---

[6]NERC's scientists have historically been very good at contributing to environmental policy, regulation, and legislation appearing as lead and contributing authors on influential reports such as chapters of the Assessment Reports of the Intergovernmental Panel for Climate Change. In focusing on the private sector, NERC is not seeking to reduce its public sector impact, but instead to increase its private sector relevance.

References

Archer, M., Bhaskar, R., Collier, A., Lawson, T., Norrie, A. (eds) (1998) *Critical Realism: Essential Readings.* London: Routledge.

Crossley, N. (2005) 'Social construction/social constructionism', in Key Concepts in Critical Social Theory. Available at: http://www.credoreference.com/entry/sageukcst/social_construction_social_constructionism (accessed 1 October 2012).

EPSRC (Engineering and Physical Sciences Research Council) (no date) 'Impact – guidance for applicants and reviewers'. Available at: http://www.epsrc.ac.uk/funding/apprev/preparing/Pages/economicimpact.aspx (accessed 7 January 2013).

ESRC (Economic and Social Research Council) (2006) 'ESRC outputs framework 2005–6'. Available at: http://www.esrc.ac.uk/ ESRCInfoCentre/Images/ESRC_Outputs_Framework-2005_06_tcm6-16579.pdf (accessed 25 August 2009).

HMSO (HM Stationery Office) (1993) 'Realising our potential: a strategy for science, engineering and technology'. Available at: http://www.official-documents.gov.uk/document/cm22/2250/2250.pdf (accessed 22 October 2011).

HM Treasury (2004) '2004–2014 science and innovation framework'. Available at: http://www.hm-treasury.gov.uk/spending_sr04_science.htm (accessed 7 October 2012).

Motluk, A. (1995) 'High price to pay for "realising our potential"' *New Scientist,* 9 September 1995: 5. Available at: http://www.newscientist.com/article/mg14719940.400-high-price-to-pay-for-realising-our-potential.html (accessed 23 October 2011).

NERC (Natural Environment Research Council) (2011) 'NERC impact report 2011: environmental science for UK economic growth and wellbeing'. Available at: http://www.nerc.ac.uk/about/perform/documents/impactreport2011.pdf (accessed 7 October 2012).

PWC (Natural Environment Research Council and PriceWaterhouse Coopers) (2006) 'Economic benefits of environmental science: a study of the economic impacts of research funded by the Natural Environment Research Council'. Available at: http://www.nerc.ac. uk/publications/corporate/economic.asp (accessed 25 August 2009).

RCUK (Research Councils UK) (no date) 'Pathways to Impact: expectations and policies', *RCUK: Knowledge Exchange and Impact.* Available at: http://www.rcuk.ac.uk/kei/impacts/Pages/expectationpolicies.aspx (accessed 23 October 2011).

RCUK (Research Councils UK), PA and SQW (2007) 'Study on the economic impact of the Research Councils'. Available at: www.rcuk.ac.uk/cmsweb/downloads/rcuk/economicimpact/recommendations.pdf (accessed 08 August 2009).

Rose, N. (1996) 'Governing "advanced" liberal democracies', in A. Barry, T. Osborne and N.S. Rose (eds), *Foucault and Political Reason: Liberalism, Neo-Liberalism and Rationalities of Government,* Chicago and London: University of Chicago Press.

Science and Technology Act (1965) London.

Warry, P. (2006) *Increasing the Economic Impact of Research Councils: Advice to the Director General of Science and Innovation, DTI, Research Council Economic Impact Group.* Department for Business, Enterprise and Regulatory Reform. Available at: www.berr.gov.uk/files/file32802.pdf (accessed 25 August 2009).

3

HOW DOES THE IMPACT AGENDA FIT WITH ATTITUDES AND ETHICS THAT MOTIVATE RESEARCH?

JENNIFER CHUBB

Key points

This interactive chapter provides:

- A discussion of the issue of motivation and its influence on research – what ethic drives particular projects?
- An outline of the discussion surrounding different 'types' of research
- An overview of different academic perceptions of impact
- An exploration of the challenges and opportunities that arise in responding to the Impact Agenda

Introduction

This chapter provides an insight into how a sample of academics view the Impact Agenda in relation to their roles. It is based upon the preliminary findings from a qualitative research project and represents the views from semi-structured interviews with academics from across all disciplines, sponsored by different Research Councils. It therefore draws together some of the themes from the previous two chapters. When quotations are used in this chapter for illustrative purposes, then the broad subject area of the respondent will be noted. From the range of responses given by academics you will see that the Impact Agenda invites healthy debate amongst the academic community. This continues the discussion raised in previous chapters.

Motivation and research

What motivates you to do research? What is it about research that drives you? Does it matter if your research has an impact and what does impact mean to you?

During the course of the research interviews the questions above were addressed. (You may feel that some of the academics have articulated views you share while others have provided counterpoints or challenges to them.)

Researchers gave a wide range of responses to questions relating to the underpinning reasons as to why it is that they do what they do, but there is a clear distinction that motivation in relation to engagement and research can be categorised in the following ways:

Intrinsically driven motivation – this refers to motivation that is driven by an interest in or passion for something for its own sake or 'in itself'; it is something that comes from within as opposed to being externally imposed. It is often seen as the 'push' that drives us to do things.

Thinking about this in relation to research and the motivations behind our endeavours, responses that indicate an intrinsic motivation for carrying out research might include:

> 'I am just so passionate about the works of Dickens' or

> 'I am curious about Baas Becking theory.'

Extrinsically driven motivation, in contrast to the latter is concerned with behaviour that is driven by the 'ends' or outcomes. Often, this is driven by external pressures as opposed to compelling internal factors. It is often seen as the 'pull' that makes us feel inclined to do things.

When thinking about impact, many researchers reported that they see this as the pursuit of a particular goal or outcome. They described their motivations in the following ways:

> 'I want to provide evidence to influence educational policy'

> 'I want to win more funding to secure an academic career.'

The Impact Agenda is therefore often associated with extrinsic motivation since it is something that is outcome focused and, to many, driven by external factors relating to performance and funding. However, for some researchers the very concept of 'making a difference', influencing and creating new products or services is felt very much to be an internal driver. So for many academics, talk of impact goes hand in hand with the very reason they are doing the research in the first place and indeed many claim that the aspiration to do excellent, curiosity-driven research need not be at odds with seeking and achieving impact. For some researchers, impact is so embedded into the heart of the research idea, from its design through to its dissemination, that they feel it is inextricably linked.

'In my field it is part and parcel of what I do' (Sciences)

ACTIVITY 3.1

Here is just a snapshot of possible drivers for carrying out research – of course there are many more. Do any of the reasons stated below resonate with you? If so, circle those that do.

make a difference	status	curiosity	advance knowledge	create new ideas
influence policy and practice	make changes, provide evidence	create new services	love of and passion for the subject	advance a career
to answer and pose new questions	find out new ways of doing things	cause an effect	contribute to the social good	engage the public
create new products	make discoveries	be the first, the expert, the best	free enquiry	academic freedom

Case studies highlighting impact as an academic motivation

The quotations below resonate with ideas presented in Chapter 1 that claim that the Impact Agenda has much in common with the way many academics think about their research.

'It is that drive of wanting to make a difference in the world – how could you not want to do that?' (Social Science)

'If there is some sense of duty or responsibility to not be totally content with the ivory tower – that people have that ethic of being an academic, then I think you can encourage people to think a different way about impact.' (Social Science)

REFLECTION POINT

What are your motivations for doing research?

Spending time reflecting on why you are doing your research will help you articulate a stronger impact narrative, whether you are discussing past or future notions of impact. Also, identifying what drives you is also likely to inspire and engage others and thus enhance the potential for collaboration and impact.

Spend some time considering what your motivations are for doing research and how you feel about impact in relation to these drivers.

Perceptions

It could be argued that the challenge comes when researchers start to associate impact with 'types' of research such as 'applied' or 'theoretical'. The perception that impact equates to 'applied research' and therefore must be diametrically opposed to any intrinsic pursuit of 'knowledge for knowledge's sake' is a view taken by some. The Research Councils explain that the Impact Agenda asks you not to change the type of research you are interested in carrying out, but to seek answers to questions about who else might feasibly be interested in the research – hence harmonising both the motivation for free enquiry with some foresight about the potential benefits of the research outside the academic community.

The following questions should be considered at the outset of any project in order to maximise its impact potential:

Who might benefit from the research (outside the academy)?

How might they benefit from the research?

What can you do to allow them the opportunity to benefit?

By building impact into the design of the project from the outset, researchers are better placed to address some of these considerations. This might require a mindset shift towards considering goals and outcomes as we have seen in Chapter 1 and in the early part of this chapter. Consider the tension that is perceived by many that the pursuit of blue-skies or curiosity-driven research cannot easily be harmonised with what might be understood as applied research. Is this necessarily the case? There are theories which can be used to illustrate that the gap between 'applied' and 'basic' (or blue skies) can be bridged and harmonised, one of which we will now discuss.

Pasteur's quadrant – applied and basic research

Donald Stokes introduced the term 'Pasteur's Quadrant' in his book *Pasteur's Quadrant: Basic Science and Technological Innovation* (Stokes, 1997). Also known as Stoke's quadrant, it outlines the ways in which the notions of pure and applied research need no longer be polarised. Indeed, the model shows that it is possible to have 'use-inspired basic research' which seeks to satisfy both the curiosity-driven, free enquiry endorsed by those who advocate blue-skies thinking with outcomes for a social/economic benefit (something we normally associate with applied research).

Pasteur's quadrant provides a framework that might reassure researchers that considering the outcomes of research and simultaneously maintaining one's own intrinsic motivations and drivers for pursuing knowledge in and for itself are not necessarily at odds with one another.

Pasteur's quadrant works in the following way. It describes how Pasteur, as one of the main founders of microbiology and whose discoveries led to the prevention of diseases, can illustrate how 'basic' and 'applied' research can be harmonised. Stokes uses the quadrant to highlight how the examples of Bohr and Edison typify the terms 'basic' and 'applied'. While Bohr's theoretical ideas about the structure of the atom have had a far-reaching effect on the scientific community generally, Edison's applied research also led to the development of devices such as the motion picture camera and the electric light bulb. Pasteur's work can be said to harmonise these ideas (which essentially reflects the notions of 'basic' and 'applied' research) through research that is 'use – inspired'. Many argue that impact is only ever the result of chance and that considering impact at the outset in this way somehow conflicts with scientific freedom and free enquiry. You might wish to consider whether you agree with this model when considering the type of research you carry out. Indeed it could be argued that the Impact Agenda actually allows us to consider the role that pure or basic research may play in being instrumental in achieving impact by working with other disciplines. Let us consider mathematics as an example:

A mathematician's perspective on impact

'Curiosity is what drives me, but as a mathematician, I am one step removed from application – but that's where the engineers and scientists come in!'

This quotation illustrates the point that for many disciplines, providing information and material for others to build on is what then generates the impact, rather than being an end in itself. An impact narrative that meaningfully articulates the journey from basic research to that which generates impact is just as valid.

ACTIVITY 3.1

Consider how you view the 'type' of research you do. Does it lend itself to responding to the Impact Agenda? If you foresee challenges, how might you overcome them? As you will read in the chapters that follow, impact need not always be generated by one individual – it is not necessarily your sole responsibility. Indeed, working in teams, partnerships and across disciplines might well be the source of your impact story. Perhaps a better way of thinking about your research is in relation to the benefits it can bring to society, if appropriate.

Remember, sponsors of research also accept cases where investigators declare that their proposed project may not generate particular socio-economic impacts (see Chapter 6) – if that is the case for your project, you must ensure you justify the reasons why that is the case. Perhaps though you might look to other disciplines to work with you to see whether there are avenues you have not yet thought about exploring.

You may have many motivations for doing research of which making an impact outside the university may only be one. However, harnessing the reasons behind your enquiry and revisiting these different drivers at different points of your career can help you to navigate this agenda.

Perspectives on impact

Many researchers believe their 'ethic' to do research in the first place is to make a difference, to consider the benefit or the social good; however, this is not always synonymous with the notion implied by the funders of research when they speak of 'impact'.

Research shows that applying a broad-brush stroke to all disciplines and defining impact in generic terms across all disciplines is not always helpful. This chapter will now consider what impact might meaningfully look like, from the broad discipline perspectives in cognate groupings, such as those from the arts and humanities, the social sciences, the applied and physical sciences and the life and earth sciences.

The term 'impact' has to mean something to people in order for it to be achieved, and the essence of the matter is that researchers are already doing such work in many interesting areas but may not necessarily associate it with the concept of impact that the funders suggest. The problem is therefore in defining it and making sense of this agenda in a way that does not compromise integrity or an academic's motivation for doing research in the first place.

So what do the Research Councils mean by impact?

A perspective from the Research Councils was provided in the previous chapter, so here I will simply provide the descriptions in Box 3.1 as a reminder.

BOX 3.1   EXCERPT FROM RCUK HTTP://WWW.RCUK.AC.UK/PAGES/HOME.ASPX

Academic impact

The demonstrable contribution that excellent research makes to academic advances, across and within disciplines, including significant advances in understanding, methods, theory and application.

Economic and societal impacts

The demonstrable contribution that excellent research makes to society and the economy. Economic and societal impacts embrace all the extremely diverse ways in which research-related knowledge and skills benefit individuals, organisations and nations by:

fostering global economic performance, and specifically the economic competitiveness of the United Kingdom,

increasing the effectiveness of public services and policy,

enhancing quality of life, health and creative output. (RCUK, 2011)

Impact can also be defined retrospectively within the context of assessment, in relation to how significant it is and how far the research influences environments outside of academia.

Do researchers interpret impact in the way the funders expect them to?

My research shows that researchers have different interpretations of impact, and the language used within the context of the Impact Agenda often confuses and complicates the issue.

The diagram below (Chubb, forthcoming thesis) emphasises how cognate groups of researchers when questioned associate their activities in terms of impact.

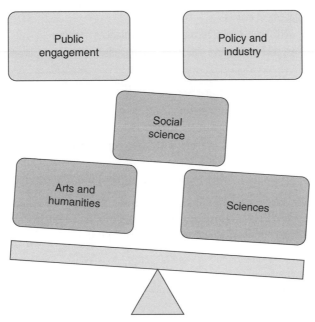

FIGURE 3.2   The balance of impact in activities

Of course, one must not assume that all researchers from these groupings necessarily agree with these categories. However, there are certainly themes emerging from research carried out with academics about how they see impact within their discipline, which demonstrate some trends in thinking which we will explore in more detail now.

Impact and the arts and humanities – looks a lot like public engagement?

Academics in the arts and humanities are embracing the culture of impact by working with a range of stakeholders to bring about cultural, economic and social enrichment. Indeed, expressing the value of the arts and humanities to the public is of growing importance. Box 3.2 details some examples of impact-generating activity cited by academics to be most relevant to the arts and humanities community.

BOX 3.2   WHAT MIGHT IMPACT ACTIVITIES LOOK LIKE TO THE ARTS AND HUMANITIES RESEARCHER?

- Public lectures
- Public engagement events
- Concerts, workshops, books, recordings, performances, media
- Partnerships: schools, creative industries, communities, museums, galleries, and more

---

The following excerpts from interviews with academic staff in the arts and humanities show the variation in views in relation to their understanding and interpretation of what is meant by the term 'impact'.

> 'Workshops? Is this actually impact or is it just public outreach?' (Arts)

> 'Philosophy does not follow fashion – any sense that what you are doing is fashionable is seen as deeply embarrassing because philosophy tries to be ahistorical – the effect is that any politically determined external pressure is bad.' (Arts)

REFLECTION POINT 〰️

What might motivate someone to do humanities research? What challenges might they face?
   Think about the arts and humanities and consider some of the ways in which its research can make a difference – how might this be achieved?

Impact and the social sciences

Academics in the social sciences are also required to consider the impact of their research. The ESRC articulate what they mean by impact in the following ways:

   Instrumental impact: 'influencing the development of policy, practice or service provision, shaping legislation, altering behaviour'.

   Conceptual impact: 'contributing to the understanding of policy issues, reframing debates'.

Capacity building impact: 'through technical and personal skill development' (ESRC, 2012).

Box 3.3 details some examples of impact-generating activity most relevant and regularly cited by academics to be of note to the social science community:

BOX 3.3   WHAT MIGHT IMPACT ACTIVITIES LOOK LIKE TO A SOCIAL SCIENTIST?

- Using evidence to inform policy
- Influencing practice in a particular field
- Using public engagement to inform and consult end users
- Partnerships: NGOs, government organisations, public, private and third sector
- Networks and consortia … and more

The following excerpts from interviews with academic staff in the social sciences provide information in relation to their understanding and interpretation of impact.

'In education, if your research isn't making an impact on your field, you ought not to be doing it.' (Education)

'You want people to know what you're doing; no point doing it otherwise.' (Social policy)

'Impact means shaping policy debate and doing that by engaging a whole range of groups that are involved in the policy making and shaping process and communicating my research and writing in ways that are useful and useable to different audiences, that's my primary focus. The academic side of that is secondary for me.' (Politics)

REFLECTION POINT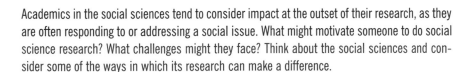

Academics in the social sciences tend to consider impact at the outset of their research, as they are often responding to or addressing a social issue. What might motivate someone to do social science research? What challenges might they face? Think about the social sciences and consider some of the ways in which its research can make a difference.

Impact and the sciences

Academics in the sciences are asked to consider the myriad ways in which scientific research can make a difference to the economy and society. Bearing in mind the issues raised within these chapters on the subject of curiosity-driven research and transformational discovery, for many scientists, considering the impact of research before a project has begun can be a challenge. This is not the case across the board however, as many consider it to be a vibrant opportunity little at odds with their scientific freedom. This section provides an insight and Box 3.4 outlines the types of impact-generating activities commonly associated with the scientific disciplines:

BOX 3.4   WHAT MIGHT IMPACT ACTIVITIES LOOK LIKE TO A SCIENTIST?

- Knowledge exchange – technology development and transfer
- Industrial collaboration
- Commercialisation
- Policy influence
- Product development

The following excerpt from interviews with academic staff in relation to their understanding and interpretation of impact provides an insight into how a scientist may perceive impact.

> 'I think the problem for us scientists is that we're always being very careful to tread on firm thick ice, firm ground, and I think when you start to talk about what you might do, you kind of know you might be extending things beyond what you're really likely to do.' (Biology)

REFLECTION POINT

Interestingly, note that from the interviews carried out with scientists that public engagement was not necessarily perceived as being associated with the Impact Agenda. Public engagement is a recognised and valid pathway to impact and should be considered when designing impact-generating activities.

What might motivate someone to do scientific research? What challenges might they face?

Think about the sciences and consider some of the ways in which scientific research can make a difference – how might this be achieved?

In summary

So far, you have been given an overview of the historical context, which underpins discussion around the emergence of the Impact Agenda. The long-standing challenge often raised when discussing the perceived conflict between the pursuit of knowledge for knowledge's sake, and the instrumentalism that the Impact Agenda implies, is an area that has received much attention in the academic community and has divided opinion in higher education.

However, when posed the question, 'what drives you to do research and what do you hope to achieve?' regardless of the kind of research being carried out (pure, applied, use-inspired), as well as wanting to advance the field of knowledge, many researchers respond in a way that suggests a broader motivation to create and contribute towards some kind of social good.

Having examined some of the case study quotations from academics who have commented on the agenda, we can also see that that the term 'impact' can be interpreted in a multitude of ways and thus causes further debate. This demonstrates that developing a clear understanding of what impact might mean to you and your discipline will be helpful in order to navigate through this culture change, particularly as an early career researcher.

One of the contentions in the previous chapter is that there is nothing new about the Impact Agenda. Indeed, it could be argued that the aspiration has always been for the role of academics within society to be understood within the context of effecting social good and change. Sir Thomas More exclaimed, 'the role of the intellectual within society is to make a difference' (in Reisz, 2012) – this statement was made shortly before his execution – (it is questionable as to whether the two were linked!). You might like to consider how far you agree with this assertion. If we take the view that the role of the academic is to make a difference, having examined your values and motivations for carrying out research you might want to consider ways in which to maximise opportunities to achieve research with impact. You could start by exploring the materials provided by your own discipline's Research Council.

The Research Councils provide case studies and toolkits to help support academics to help researchers to articulate and demonstrate ways in which their research can make a difference outside the academic community. The councils include:

Arts and Humanities Research Council
Biotechnology and Biological Sciences Research Council
Engineering and Physical Sciences Research Council
Economic and Social Research Council
Medical Research Council
Natural Environment Research Council
Science and Technology Facilities Council
You might then peruse the rest of the book for further ideas.

References

Chubb, J.A. (forthcoming thesis) 'The impact agenda and academics' perception of their roles: perspectives from the UK and Australia'.

ESRC (2012) 'What is impact?' Available at http://www.esrc.ac.uk/funding-and-guidance/tools-and-resources/impact-toolkit/what-how-and-why/what-is-research-impact.aspx

More, T., quoted by Andrew Pettigrew, in Reisz, M. (2012) 'Engage with business to make a difference,' *Times Higher education*, July. Available at www.timeshighereducation.co.uk/420427.article.

RCUK (2011) 'RCUK impact requirements frequently asked questions'. Available at http://rcuk.ac.uk/documents/impacts/RCUKImpactFAQ.pdf

Stokes, F.D. (1997) *Pasteur's Quadrant: Basic Science and Technological Innovation*. Washington, DC: Brookings Institution Press, p. 73.

4

WHAT ARE THE DIFFERENT CHARACTERISTICS OF RESEARCH IMPACT?

JO LAKEY, GEOFF RODGERS AND ROSA SCOBLE

Key points

- Current thinking on the characteristics of impact based on disciplinary differences and research activities
- How might you understand your impact and how it might be interpreted in assessment by funding bodies?
- What you should think about when describing your routes to impact in a disciplinary context?
- How you can capture and present all the dimensions of your impact?

Introduction

The Impact Agenda has dominated academic debate in the past few years and, in the UK, the introduction of the assessment of impact into the Research Excellence Framework (REF2014) has made it a critical issue for academic leaders across the sector. However, this is not just a national agenda but has been introduced, whether explicitly or implicitly, internationally and by all types of funding organisations.

The debate will probably never be settled about whether the emphasis on impact is 'good' or 'bad' for the future of academic research, with arguments and counter-arguments on both sides. Nevertheless, as an individual researcher, this cannot be ignored; therefore, it is essential to be able to understand and articulate the impact of your research in a way that makes sense to all stakeholders: the public, funders, potential new employers, colleagues and senior academic management. It has to be noted that the ability to articulate the 'lack' of impact is probably as important and that, therefore, it is essential to have an understanding of how the particular characteristics of your research might hinder an easy path to impact.

This chapter will give you a theoretical framework as well as practical ideas on how you might characterise your impact. One of the challenges is to think about all the ways your research has had, or might have, impact and this chapter will provide you with an array of descriptors that you could choose to use within the context of your research to build your case for impact.

Impact characteristics

To understand the whole process of the creation of impact, it is important to look at the fundamental building blocks: the influence of time, the type of research activity and the disciplinary context.

The notion of time

For blue-skies research with high academic significance it is only a question of time before it generates societal impact. This chapter will include examples of discoveries that initially did not appear to have any socio-economic impact, but eventually have come to transform our world (see also Chapter 5).

Donovan (2011) describes research impact as part of a social contract that exists between science and society, embracing broader social, cultural, environmental and economic returns. The 'social contract' means that it is highly likely that academic research will generate some form of impact outside academia. Most research questions are framed through the desire to solve a specific problem or to answer a specific question, both of which can benefit society. As research becomes increasingly applied, involving end users from the beginning, the time-lag between research and impact is becoming shorter, where historically it has taken time for the impact of research to reach beyond academia. There are disciplines where research will always take more time to reach beyond academia and generate impact, the theoretical sciences for example. In the same way that a product can take many years to make it from design to manufacturing to market, the pathway from research to impact can also take time, as research is published and then disseminated before being picked up outside academia.

Martin (2011) describes the difficulty of assessing impact – 'the fact that it is often indirect, partial, opaque and long-term'. The long-term aspect of impact generation has made it necessary to include research which is up to 15 years old in the impact submission to the REF2014, and in some cases even older research (up to 25 years for Architecture) will be allowed. The REF2014 guidance also allows for impacts to be submitted at any stage of development, allowing 'interim' impacts to be submitted. This gives institutions the potential to submit impacts to subsequent research assessments as they grow and develop over time. For example, research which influences policy-makers can be submitted as an interim impact, with the potential for submission to the next exercise if a law or policy has been altered, because the impact will grow as the law or policy is implemented.

ACTIVITY 4.1   REFLECTION ON THE IMPACT OF FAMOUS RESEARCH

Think about Newton (Law of Gravity), Einstein (Relativity) and Watson and Crick (DNA structure). Do you think their research was considered impactful at the time? How long did it take for the full impact to be acknowledged? What was the time lag?

Research taxonomy

The Frascati Manual (OECD, 2002) describes the different ways in which research fields can be categorised. It also provides definitions of the different fields of science and of the difference between basic and applied research. Examples of how research within these disciplinary categories generates impact, and the characterisation of this impact, will help researchers understand what might be expected in their own discipline.

The Frascati Manual is a document that formalises the collection and methodology for the survey of Research and Development at a national level for the Organisation for Economic Co-operation and Development (OECD). The current (sixth) version of the Frascati Manual was published in 2002. It is seen as a primary source for the definition of terms about research, research organisations, disciplines and activities and the definition of 'research' is the one adopted by HEFCE in all research assessment exercises, and it is shown in Box 4.1 (see also OECD, 2002: 31).

However, in the context of the pathways from original research to impact on the classification of the research activity demonstrates a well-established view of the likelihood of research going beyond just the creation of knowledge. The Frascati Manual classifies research into three different activities, also included in Box 4.1.

BOX 4.1   COMMON DEFINITIONS OF RESEARCH

Research and experimental development (R&D) comprises creative work undertaken on a systematic basis in order to increase the stock of knowledge, including knowledge of man, culture and society, and the use of this stock of knowledge to devise new applications.

Basic research is experimental or theoretical work undertaken primarily to acquire new knowledge of the underlying foundation of phenomena and observable facts, without any particular application or use in view.

Applied research is also original investigation undertaken in order to acquire new knowledge. It is, however, directed primarily towards a specific practical aim or objective.

Experimental development is systematic work, drawing on existing knowledge gained from research and/or practical experience, which is directed to producing new materials, products or devices, to installing new processes, systems and services, or to improving substantially those already produced or installed.

It is quite apparent that in this particular view 'basic research' has little chance of making any direct impact. However, when combined with the previous 'notion of time' one can see how 'basic research' can make an everlasting impact on the world's future developments.

Impact types

There are many ways to define the types of impacts of research. This section will draw on both the literature and on more recent developments, such as the REF2014, to illustrate the different ways impact types can be defined. It will have examples of types of impact and contain exercises on 'defining the impact'.

The Frascati Manual concentrates very much on the economic benefits of research and, whilst a useful tool, does not address the wider social benefits of research.

Again, the Payback framework (Buxton and Hanney, 1996) looks at the return on investment of healthcare research, specifically the economic benefits. The framework details five payback categories:

- Knowledge production
- Research targeting and capacity building
- Informing policy and product development
- Health and health sector benefits
- Wider economic benefits

Godin and Doré (2005) discuss the impacts of *science*, citing Salter and Martin's six identified categories for the benefits derived from publicly funded research (2001):

- Increasing the stock of useful knowledge
- Training skilled graduates
- Creating new scientific instrumentation and methodologies
- Forming networks and stimulating social interactions
- Increasing the capacity for scientific and technological problem-solving
- Creating new firms

However, Godin and Doré recognise that, like the Frascati Manual, these six categories focus almost exclusively on economic benefits of research, and do not cover the range of benefits which research offers to society. Their own study identified a much broader range of impacts (Table 4.1).

ACTIVITY 4.2 DEFINING YOUR OWN RESEARCH

Think about your research and define it in terms of one of the three activities presented in the Frascati Manual. Would you be able to 'look into the future' and see which of the types of impact proposed in Table 4.1 it may achieve? If yours is basic research can you envisage any type of impact?

TABLE 4.1 Godin and Doré's typology of categories of impact

Science	Organisation
• Knowledge	• Planning
• Research activities	• Work organisation
• Training	• Administration
	• Human resources
Technology	
• Products and processes	**Health**
• Services	• Public health
• Know-how	• Health system
Economy	**Environment**
• Production	• Management of natural resources and the
• Financing	environment
• Investments	• Climate and meteorology
• Commercialisation	
• Budget	**Symbolic**
Culture	• Legitimacy/credibility/visibility
	• Notoriety
• Knowledge	
• Know-how	**Training**
• Attitudes	
• Values	• Curricula
	• Pedagogical tools
Society	• Qualifications
	• Graduates
• Welfare	• Entrance into the job market
• Discourses and actions of groups	• Fitness of training/work
	• Career
Policy	• Use of acquired knowledge
• Policy-makers	
• Citizens	
• Public programmes	
• National security	

Assessment of impact

From the literature, it is clear that impact is subjective, and dependent on audience. It can be used as a measure of return on investment from research, as well as an indicator of innovation and economic development or social benefit. It is therefore important to understand the purpose of the impact assessment when defining the types of impact. Specific disciplines are likely to have their own forms of impact, and impacts which are common in one discipline may be unheard of in another (for example impact arising from the design of a new product is less likely to occur in the humanities, just as impacts on public policy are much more likely to arise from research in social sciences than from research in chemistry or physics).

REF2014 (administered by the UK funding council HEFCE) is currently the first attempt to assess and fund research impact. Impact counts for 20 per cent of the profile in the assessment and, very probably, will increase in future assessments. HEFCE defined impact as 'an effect on, change or benefit to the economy, society, culture, public policy or services, health, the environment or quality of life beyond academia' (HEFCE, 2011). Impact for REF2014 included (but was not limited to) an effect on, change or benefit to:

- the activity, attitude, awareness, behaviour, capacity, opportunity, performance, policy, practice, process or understanding;
- of an audience, beneficiary, community, constituency, organisation or individuals;
- in any geographic location whether locally, regionally, nationally or internationally.

Impact included the reduction or prevention of harm, risk, cost or other negative effects.

For REF2014, impacts on research, or the advancement of academic knowledge within the higher education sector (whether in the UK or internationally) were excluded, as were impacts on students, teaching or other activities within the submitting university. Other impacts within the HE sector, including on teaching or students, were included where they extended significantly beyond the submitting university.

Impact for REF2014 was assessed in terms of its 'reach and significance' regardless of the geographic location in which it occurred.

For the purposes of REF2014, it was important to distinguish between the dissemination of research and instances where actual impact has occurred. Donovan (2008) discusses the 'pushmi-pullyu' aspect of Australia's RQF, which can also be applied to the impact requirement of the REF2014, where dissemination consists of academic institutions 'pushing' their research and where a user group engaging with that research creates a 'pull' whereby impacts can occur.

It is important to recognise that for most impacts there are likely to be multiple factors and contributions. It is unusual for an impact to be the result of a single piece of research. Most will be the result of a body of research, performed by multiple researchers in multiple institutions. It is for this reason that HEFCE asked for evidence of the link between the research of a particular institution and the impact as part of the REF2014 submission.

Impacts can therefore be broken down into three broad areas:

- impacts which were inevitable and would have happened without the input of research;
- impacts which occurred because of a range of inputs from research;
- impacts which occurred because of one piece of research.

For REF2014, the four individual assessment panels provided details of the types of impacts that they expected to see. These are displayed in Table 4.2.

Whilst the types of impact did not differ hugely between panels, it is interesting to note the differences between the panels and the impacts that they were expecting to see. Panel C was the least prescriptive, encouraging institutions to submit impact case studies 'in any sphere consistent with the general guidance' (HEFCE, 2012).

Economic impacts

There is a huge range of economic and commercial impacts generated from research, from the revenue growth generated from new products and services, or through improved business practices to increased investment in businesses, and the collaborations which can be generated between business and academia. What is distinct about economic impacts is that (for the most part) they are quantifiable and the contribution of a particular researcher or piece of research is clear and measurable.

Environmental impacts

Environmental issues are becoming increasingly important, and environmental benefits from research range from influence on environmental policy, to processes and services which increase sustainability encouraging behavioural changes and reducing pollution and consumption of natural resources.

Social impacts

Social impacts cover a range of benefits to society which focus on social welfare, social equity, improve public services and training of practitioners.

Health impacts

Benefits to public health include improvements to patient care, influence on clinical policy and, through improvements in patient care, the resultant improvements in quality of life and lives saved.

TABLE 4.2   HEFCE, REF2014: Types of impact by disciplinary groups

Panel A	Panel C
Clinical Medicine; Public Health, Health Services and Primary Care; Allied Health Professions, Dentistry, Nursing and Pharmacy; Psychology, Psychiatry and Neuroscience; Biological Sciences; Agriculture, Veterinary and Food Science	Architecture, Built Environment and Planning; Geography, Environmental Studies and Archaeology; Economics and Econometrics; Business and Management Studies; Law; Politics and International Studies; Social Work and Social Policy; Sociology; Anthropology and Development Studies; Education; Sports-Related Studies

Panel A	Panel C
• Economic impacts	• Culture
• Commercial impacts	• The economy
• Impacts on public policy and services	• The environment
• Impacts on society, culture and creativity	• Health
• Health and welfare impacts	• Public policy, law and services
• Production impacts	• Society
• Impacts on practitioners and services	
• Impacts on the environment	
• Impacts on international development	

Panel B	Panel D
Earth Systems and Environmental Sciences; Chemistry; Physics; Mathematical Sciences; Computer Science and Informatics; Aeronautical, Mechanical, Chemical and Manufacturing Engineering; Electrical and Electronic Engineering; Metallurgy and Materials; Civil and Construction Engineering; General Engineering	Area Studies; Modern Languages; English Language and Literature; History; Classics; Philosophy; Theology and Religious Studies; Art and Design: History, Practice and Theory; Music, Drama, Dance and Performing Arts; Communication, Cultural and Media Studies; Library and Information Management

Panel B	Panel D
• Economic impacts	• Civil society
• Impacts on public policy and services	• Cultural life
• Impacts on society, culture and creativity	• Economic prosperity
• Health impacts	• Education
• Impacts on practitioners and professional services	• Policy making
• Impacts on the environment	• Public discourse
	• Public services

Cultural impacts

Research can improve public engagement with science and heritage, and can lead to changes in cultural practice and collaborations with cultural bodies to educate and change attitudes to important issues.

Moving down through the non-economic types of impact, it becomes evident that most types of impact are difficult to quantify and measure. It can be also difficult to trace the route from research to impact, particularly in areas which are subject to multiple contributions from researchers and other bodies.

Routes from discipline to impact

This section will bring together the work in the previous three sections. It will trace the main routes from specific discipline categories, through time, to the different types of impact. Recognising the complexities of impact and that routes are not always linear, this section will explore the relationships between researchers and impact partners and will give examples of how users can be engaged and involved throughout a project to maximise the possibilities for impact. Examples of routes and exercises on 'trace the route' will help the researcher understand routes not only within their discipline but also the wider research landscape.

Socio-economic impact can arise from many types of research and can take many routes from the initial research to the impact on a user or user community.

Linear routes to impact usually occur when a particular product or service is specifically designed to benefit a user community. There is a clearly traceable route from the research, through publication of results, to manufacturing and sale of the item and thence to the benefit that it provides. When the route to the impact is linear, there may be several different types of impact which arise from the example of a specifically designed product or service. For example, there may be quality of life benefits to the users, environmental impacts from products or services which use more carbon-friendly materials, economic benefits from the sale of items. These impacts are more quantifiable because concrete numbers can be applied to these benefits, and the impact story is easily described.

These routes are exemplified in Figure 4.1a, which shows research originating within academia (at point R0), being exploited and modified by further research within academia and then reaching the users at point U0.

Figure 4.1b shows another linear route from research to impact, where research is used by knowledge brokers (professional bodies, learned societies, lobbying groups, etc.) to reach user communities and starts to have

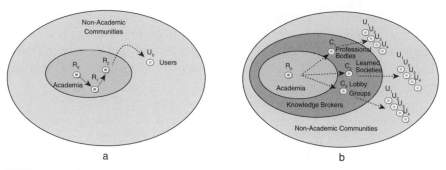

FIGURE 4.1 Schematic representation of examples of impact diffusion

impact outside academia. These types of routes to impact tend to be in disciplines like social sciences, where research is used to influence policy making, or is distributed to practitioners via knowledge brokers. Impact which arises from these routes is generally less quantifiable, since it is much more difficult to quantify impacts such as influence on policy, although changes in practice can be measured where data is available, for example the number of practitioners affected by changes in practice guidelines can be further quantified by the number of patients who would be affected.

Non-linear routes to impact can occur when research activity involves the user community throughout the process, from project design to the conclusion of the project. Continuous feedback throughout the research process may lead to changes being made to practice or to policy which have an immediate impact on the user community. Thus impact is occurring simultaneously with the research. An example of this is a project undertaken with a local council's mental health services. Feedback from the service users during the research demonstrated a clear gap in services, and the provision of resources by the council to provide additional services. The impact on the user community was immediately felt, before the study was completed or the findings published. Another example might be the impact felt by a small number of users, perhaps those participating in a study, where benefits are experienced during the research. These may be considered interim impacts, as the 'reach' of the impact (as defined by HEFCE for REF2014) is relatively small, but can be reported as quality of life or health benefits nonetheless.

Non-linear routes to impact also include instances where research has been exploited in a different discipline and has produced impacts which were totally unexpected and unforeseen at the time that the original research was carried out. Often these impacts will be difficult to trace back to the original research, as the exploiting researcher or company may not reference the original research, and/or the original researcher may not be aware of activities generated after the publication of their findings, particularly if such activity happens years after the original research was carried out.

For impact to occur, there needs to be some form of engagement with a user community. In some disciplines this is endemic, as research is largely applied and users become partners in research, with projects specifically designed to create some form of benefit. These benefits may be experienced through improved policy making, improved product design, quality of life or health benefits or improved awareness of particular issues. However, for some disciplines, which historically have been further removed from their users, relationships are often formed after the research has been conducted, through dissemination and engagement events. It can be difficult to make an impression in an over-crowded market place, particularly in those disciplines with many academics in several institutions all clamouring to engage the same set of users and make them aware of their findings. Engaging users from the outset and keeping them involved with the research process ensures that research reaches the non-academic community and that researchers are able to be responsive to the needs of the user community, enabling their research to make a real, measurable impact.

Capturing and presenting impact

As illustrated in this chapter, there are many characteristics, some of which are discipline dependent, that might support or hinder socio-economic impact. However, and in most instances, it is important to spend some time in either planning for impact or finding ways to describe it.

As a last 'tip' and taking into consideration what has been described above, one way to simplify the description and planning of research impact is to answer a few simple questions.

Questions

    i. Whose problems are you trying to solve?
   ii. Who are your user communities?
  iii. How might your research be of interest to a more 'applied' discipline closer to user communities?

And now, for each question, a few simple answers.

i. **Problems**

   a. Economic growth/profit
   b. Efficient/effective processes
   c. Cultural enrichment
   d. Quality of life
   e. Health
   f. Democratic debates

ii. **Users/interest groups**

   a. Industry
   b. Service industry
   c. Policy-makers
   d. Lobbying groups
   e. Learned societies
   f. Communities
   g. Public health

iii. **Other disciplines**

   a. Technologies
   b. Social sciences
   c. Health

ACTIVITY 4.3   TRACING YOUR ROUTE

As a last exercise, try to define the problem you are currently exploring in terms of questions i and ii. If your research doesn't fit into any of these categories, can you answer question iii? Are there any other disciplines that might make use of your research and have some form of impact?

Conclusion

There are many ways in which impact can be characterised: by the nature of the underpinning research activity, the type of impacts, the type of user communities, etc. Some of these taxonomies might be more relevant to one researcher than another. However, the identification of these characteristics can help develop a narrative on the journey from the underpinning research to impact.

At a time where impact has a substantial influence on funding, the ability to understand and describe its nature and characteristics will be an important asset for any early career researcher.

References

Buxton, M. and Hanney, S. (1996) 'How can payback from health services research be assessed?' *Journal of Health Services Research and Policy*, 1 (1): 35–43.

Donovan, C. (2008) 'The Australian Research Quality Framework: a live experiment in capturing the social, economic, environmental, and cultural returns of publicly funded research', in C.L.S. Coryn and M. Scriven (eds), *Reforming the Evaluation of Research: New Directions for Evaluation,* 118: 47–60.

Donovan, C. (2011) 'State of the art in assessing research impact: introduction to a special issue', *Research Evaluation*, 20 (3): 175–9.

Gartner, R., Cox, M., Clements, A. and Joerg, B. (2010) 'Impact indicators/measures: a survey of existing work'. Available at http://mice.cerch.kcl.ac.uk/?page_id=42 (accessed 1 August 2012).

Godin, B. and Doré, C. (2005) 'Measuring the impacts of science: beyond the economic dimension', INRS Urbanisation, Culture et Société. Paper presented at: 1) Helsinki Institute for Science and Technology Studies, HIST Lecture, 24 August 2007, Helsinki, Finland; 2) International Conference, 'Science Impact – Rethinking the Impact of Basic Research on Society and the Economy', organised by the Austrian Science Fund (FWF) and the European Science Foundation (ESF), 10–11 May 2007, Vienna.

HEFCE (2011) *Assessment Framework and Guidance on Submissions*, REF 02.2011, Bristol: Higher Education Funding Council for England.

HEFCE (2012) *Panel Criteria and Working Methods*, REF 01.2012. Bristol: Higher Education Funding Council for England.

Martin, B. (2011) 'The research excellence framework and the "impact agenda": are we creating a Frankenstein monster?' *Research Evaluation*, 20 (3): 247–54.

OECD (2002) 'Frascati manual'. Available at http://www.oecdbookshop.org/oecd/display.asp?lang=EN&sf1=identifiers&st1=922002081p1

Salter, A.J. and Martin, B.R. (2001) 'The economic benefits of publicly funded basic research: a critical review', *Research Policy*, 30: 509–32.

5

WHEN MIGHT RESEARCH IMPACT BE APPARENT?

CHRISTOPHER WOOD

Key points

- When we might expect to see the impact of research
- The difference between looking 'forwards' or 'backwards' for assessing researcher impact
- What delayed impact is and how it can affect our understanding
- When it is best to measure the impact of research
- When we would expect to see the impact of developing researchers

Introduction

The routes and mechanisms through which research is communicated to places where it can make a difference, namely have 'impact', are many and varied. Additionally, the ways in which research is then used are also complex. Research may directly influence changes in policy, practices and behaviour. Or it may, in more subtle ways, change people's knowledge, understanding and attitudes towards social issues.

However, knowing *where* to look for research impacts (who the research users are); knowing *when* to look for these impacts (how long it takes for research to take effect?); and knowing *how* to assess the specific contributions made by the research (whether the research really was the key factor in any changes observed?) are key questions when assessing impact.

In this chapter we are going to concentrate on *when* we would expect to see the impacts of research, the different ways of looking at impact (either forwards or backwards in time), effects of delayed impact and when we would expect to see the impacts of individual researcher development.

When should we measure impact?

When we should measure the impact of research, or when we should expect to witness the impact of research is an interesting, and somewhat, complex question.

Depending upon what the investigators' requirements are, the question can be considered in one of two contexts:

   i.   If the impact measure is to be used to plan for proportionate and/or directed activity, the assessment of the impact should be commensurate with the size of the original research programme. In other words, when to measure the impact relates to specific goals which are usually necessary for the guidance of important decisions (such as resource allocation).
   ii. The question can be a simple 'time-frame' investigation of when we should expect to see impact (or expect it to be interpreted). That is, how soon after completion of the research should any impact assessment be carried out or measure expected? (see Reflection Point 5.1.)

In this first part of the chapter we will consider the nature of research impacts that could be examined. Some research is explicitly related to 'tactical impacts' that ought to be readily assessed in the short to medium term, to help with decision-making and planning, whereas other desired impacts such as a 'development of a research-minded culture that can affect strategy' require a far longer perspective.

REFLECTION POINT 5.1

Sir John Gurdon has been working on finding a breakthrough treatment for life threatening diseases since 1962. However, it was not until 2012 that his work was recognised by the world. In late 2012, Gurdon and his collaborating researcher Shinya Yamanaka were awarded the Nobel Prize for their work in stem-cell therapy. Their findings carry significant implications and have laid the foundations for this area of regenerative medicine. However, there was a time when these two researchers had faced difficulties in making their work known. Particularly for Sir John Gurdon, this has been an extrapolated example in how it can take considerable time for the 'impact' of research to become apparent and accepted. Few of us can project what impact our research might have in 50 years' time, though it is heartening to dream this might happen, so we will concentrate on shorter time frames in this chapter.

One also needs to consider the need to find suitable measurements (such as successful communication and research awareness amongst potential target audiences) when, or if, the impacts of the research under scrutiny are simply too diffuse or 'distant' (in time) to be readily assessed.

It is important to remember that 'it is simply not enough to consider only when to assess impacts but also how to measure them' (this is discussed more fully in later sections of Chapters 7 and 8).

What do we need to consider when we are looking for impact?

In attempting to understand the impact of research, *baseline data* can be essential to our understanding; it can enable reflection and informed change (see Chapter 7). Often, however, baseline data is simply not available or has not been measured (for example, if an agenda is implemented at short notice). Whenever and wherever possible, baseline data should be collected while efforts should be made to attain baseline data if it is not readily available (see Reflection Point 5.2).

REFLECTION POINT 5.2 〰

In 2011 the Research Councils UK published a range of impact reports in an attempt to help define the many aspects of research impact and detail some baseline measures. It is hoped that, by encouraging the collection of data of this type in the future, attempts to measure the impact of both research and researcher development can be more easily made. It might be useful for you to begin to consider what baseline data might aid you in measuring developments to be expected from your future research.

It can be seen from Reflection Point 5.2, that it is important to understand the need to gather information which is related specifically to changes that have been implemented related to the area under investigation (in this example research funding). If targeted improvements are to be considered, such analysis needs to take place alongside the general impact of research *per se*. Similarly, at a higher level, research funders could also benefit from sharing data with each other, within a commonly agreed framework (see final section of this chapter and Appendix I). This will undoubtedly aid funders and policy-makers (as well as researchers in general) to further understand the impact of the research they are interested in.

However, it is important to fully understand what your data means. It can be relatively simple to collect data, but this data has to be meaningful and focused on answering your enquiry questions. The questions need to elicit answers that are of value to all those involved within your study; otherwise they can confuse or overwhelm. Thus the starting point for assessing research impact must be good enquiry questions – see Box 5.1.

BOX 5.1 GOOD EXAMPLES OF ENQUIRY QUESTIONS

- What is it that you want to learn about?
- On which processes are you basing your enquiry?
- Over what time period?
- Are the results of impact measurement to:
  - effect leadership?
  - maintain and enhance happier and more productive staff?
  - achieve a more joined-up provision?
  - garner greater community engagement?
  - provide improved outcomes for researchers in general?

Just as early career researchers cannot improve their research standing without constructive feedback from their supervisors or principal investigators (for example, they need to gather data about their own practices, strengths and weakness), so do more established researchers and institutions. There has to be feedback and data upon which to reflect in order to make evidence-informed changes. This powerful combination of receiving feedback on whether you are making impact in research, and the collation of baseline (or on-going) data collection enables stories to be told about research and its impact at local, national and international levels.

Baseline data

Baseline data should be used to produce evidence that would persuade 'sceptics' (many of whom will be outside the immediate agenda and probably unaware of it) that the approach taken has been worthwhile and will have impact (see Box 5.2).

BOX 5.2   'BASELINE' QUESTIONS TO BE ASKED WHEN THINKING ABOUT IMPACT

What was our starting point?
How far did we progress?
Which direction did we take?
Where do we want to be and how will we know when we have got there?

It is also important to remember that existing data (be produced contextually or publicly available) should be collated and archived in ways that make it easy to revisit (see Reflection Point 5.2). At the same time, local data collection can also serve as an important aspect of assessing impact, particularly at the individual or institutional level.

Suitable indicators for measurement that are adaptable over time

Indicators need to demonstrably show progress towards locally, or more wide-reaching, objectives. They need to produce data that is 'fit for purpose'. These indicators need to do three things: assess, communicate and lead to change (see Chapters 7 and 8).

A good example of an effective indicator is something that can be measured, for instance 'how researcher development funding has affected postgraduate doctoral researcher completion rates' since levels of funding can be measured and completion rates logged against these levels. More generally, levels of application of an intervention can be correlated with levels of output. It is worth noting that data has little value if it is not of specific use to its stakeholders. As such, the process of collecting the data needs to be valued and appreciated. Users simply do not use data if they do not find it useful or indispensable. Additionally, data that can be adapted over time allows for innovation, which in turn can be used to measure how the activity has been impactful.

Thus far, we have considered what factors should be considered in assessing impact over time, the effect of baseline data considerations and how this can 'focus minds' to understand the impact, not only on possible policy decisions but also to the individual researchers. The following section will consider two distinct ways of anticipating impact, which are primarily affected by baseline data considerations.

Should we look forward or back?

While considering the assessment of impact there are essentially one of two options to choose from. The assessor can either look forward in time from the starting point (i.e. a prospective measurement), or they can look back, retrospectively, at what has happened in the past. In this section we will scrutinise both of these modes of assessment, examine their differences and consider the advantages and disadvantages of taking each particular approach.

Prospective measurements

Prospective measurements are those that follow a group of similar individuals (a cohort), or monitor the effects of distinct policies, or experimental results over a period of time. They can show how key factors within cohorts/policies/experiments can affect the rates of outcomes under examination, which may affect research impact (see Reflection Point 5.3).

Prospective studies can be important when considering the impact of research activities, due to the lag which is inherent in obtaining research data. There can often be a considerable time lapse before research produces results that are of value to a wide audience (see Reflection Point 5.1). In addition, due to the inherently complex nature of research, precise and predictable results (and hence their outcomes or 'impact') are often difficult to determine, or indeed, predict (see later in this chapter).

REFLECTION POINT 5.3

A cohort of early career researchers who vary in their levels of skills development activity could be used as an example of prospective analysis; this, for example, could be used to test the hypothesis that researchers who attend relevant training will complete their research with more ease and have an enhanced future research profile, better subsequent career development and increased overall research impact. Can you think of an example in your own field that is similar to this, with different potential impacts over time?

Cohort studies

Prospective cohort studies typically produce evidence that is more valued than retrospective studies, primarily because they can be 'tailored' for investigation. They also have the option of collecting important contextual data which may have been omitted from previous studies. One of the key advantages of prospective cohort studies is they can help determine more accurately which aspects of impact will become apparent; they are longitudinal observations over time. The rigour of the results can be strengthened if measurements are conducted at regular time intervals, so that results are entirely comparable.

Case studies

In almost direct contrast to cohort studies are the more traditional case studies. In these studies, different groups of individuals are observed (usually alongside a 'control' group) until they develop an outcome of interest. The level of impact can then be attributed to how frequently the outcome is evident (or, for a quantitative measure, the levels of impact) in each of the observed groups.

The results of measuring impact from prospective studies can be used to measure and inform, and hence are particularly good for constructing or adapting policy or procedures. They can also be used to identify better alternatives if the impact assessment is not satisfactory or not delivering on policy decisions.

Prospective measurements are dependent upon having good control processes or groups. For some measures of impact (for example, how UK research expenditure compares internationally), baseline data is readily available; for others (for example, the effect of the research skills agenda on early career researcher employment and competitiveness) baseline data is either scarce or simply non-existent. In the latter case, you can only really consider a prospective analysis (see Box 5.3 for considerations with prospective measurements).

BOX 5.3   IMPORTANT CONSIDERATIONS FOR PROSPECTIVE MEASUREMENTS

- The technical limitations to the measurement
- Although baseline data is less critical, it can be useful if available
- The feasibility of changes to be considered
- Measurements that are relevant to capacity building
- Personal development considerations to be addressed (see final section).

Of course, the obvious benefit of prospective measurements is that you are 'looking forward'. Thus such an examination is therefore particularly useful for 'capacity building'.

Retrospective measurements

Retrospective measurements (looking back) are very appropriate when we have to work to a pre-assigned programme (for example of expansion or for improvement) and/or there is extensive existing data (a good baseline). With sufficient baseline data, analysis can be conducted (using, for instance, regression, randomisation and variation measures). There are several considerations to be made when considering a retrospective analysis (see Box 5.4).

BOX 5.4   IMPORTANT CONSIDERATIONS FOR RETROSPECTIVE ANALYSIS

- What are you to looking to do with the analysis (expansion or improvement)?
- What baseline data already exists (to work from)?
- Retrospective analysis is particularly useful for making strategic judgements/informing policy decisions.

Prospective vs retrospective assessments of impact

As mentioned above, prospective and retrospective analyses have different strengths and weaknesses. In this section we will consider these differences in more detail.

The major strength of a prospective assessment of impact is the accuracy of data collection with regard to policy, stakeholders and endpoints. However, this is often realised at the cost of an inevitable loss of efficiency, for this design is both expensive and time-consuming due to the usually long follow-up or lag period. In direct contrast, retrospective design can be a very time-efficient and elegant way of answering new questions with existing data, if it exists.

When measuring impact it is certainly useful to build in appropriate measures to new research plans in order for detailed prospective measurement to be completed. Indeed many current funding sources now require this level of detail to be included in applications (see Chapter 6). However, if there is sufficient baseline data to determine impact, retrospective assessments are useful to determine future avenues of research investigation or investment.

Delayed impact

When considering when one might expect to see impact from research activities (particularly when looking prospectively), it is impossible to ignore the fact alluded to above that in almost all aspects of research there is an element of delay before the impact will become apparent. In this section of the chapter we will look at what types of issue can cause delay and how this affects impact assessment.

REFLECTION POINT 5.4 〰️

Consider, for example, current research activities at the Large Hadron Collider built by the European Organisation for Nuclear Research. This research is focused on testing the theories of both particle and high-energy physics and has gained considerable international attention and repute. It is expected to address some of the most fundamental questions of physics and advance our most basic understandings of the laws of nature. However, the true 'impact' of this research may only become apparent in many decades to come. Moreover, there are already emerging many other 'impacts' of this research that were simply not envisaged initially, for example in relation to computing and medicine (see Goldfarb, 2011).

What do we mean by delay?

There are essentially two definitions of the word 'delay': to 'defer' or to 'impede progress'. When measuring impact we need to bear both of these definitions in mind. For example, it may be politically astute to defer certain aspects of research based on strategic aims. However, by far the most common source of delay when measuring the impact of research activities are various impediments which mean that the research is slow to reach implementation stages and therefore the impact of the research may not be apparent for some considerable time (see Reflection Point 5.4). Furthermore, dissemination of research itself takes time, thus final implementation of the results of the research may take place some considerable time after the commencement of the initial investigation (see Reflection Point 5.1).

It is also worth remembering that, in many instances, what has been learnt from the research setting is often not implemented into daily practice. Therefore the perceived impact of the research can easily be diminished (see Reflection Point 5.5). Moreover, it is becoming less common for researchers and potential beneficiaries of the research to be in close proximity. Compiling a list of 'impacts' that involve research where the practitioners are more remote from the research (an increasingly predominant mode of practice) can be difficult.

REFLECTION POINT 5.5 〰️

A recent review of published studies on the quality of healthcare received by Americans, for example, has found that only about three out of five patients with chronic conditions received the recommended care for a range of economic or strategic political reasons. Thus the potential impact of the initial research (and subsequent recommendations) was severely diminished (see McGlynn, 2003). Consider how the impact of your research might be diminished because of distance, or number of steps in the chain, or politico-economic factors between researcher and potential beneficiary.

Indeed, there are many 'hurdles' in terms of observing demonstrable impact, despite a wide range of strategies for implementing research into practice. These include: policies that enhance the collation of 'impactful' research so that individual impacts are hidden or obscured; local and national drivers may be focused on other areas of impact; and a lack interest in the research area or greater focus on other areas which have higher strategic priorities.

The success of demonstrating impact may be also influenced by the research environment, the researchers, organisational factors, or whether there is desire for behavioural or organisational change. Of course, all of the above will affect the time at which impact is observed, or if it is indeed seen at all.

When considering when the impact of research may become apparent, there are several items to consider in relation to the above context and these are listed in Box 5.5.

BOX 5.5   THINGS TO CONSIDER WHEN THINKING ABOUT *WHEN* IMPACT MIGHT BE DEMONSTRATED

- How the key individuals and stakeholders may affect measurement
- How long it will take to build the evidence base to demonstrate impact
- The credibility of the issue/problem (i.e. a historical perspective)
- Whether there is a critical time for the impact to be apparent (especially when it may affect policy decisions).

In this section we have begun to uncover some of the possible reasons for the delay in observing (and therefore assessing) impact. We will now look at what the significance of delay in observing impact can mean.

What is the significance of delay?

The delay of impact can be related to both specific research activities and individual researcher development. The effects upon the development of researchers will be more fully addressed later. First, we will consider the effects of delay upon the impact assessment of research activities, *per se*.

It is often difficult to make decisions that are 'timely', as the results of the research may be apparent either too late or, indeed, after the issue has been addressed elsewhere. When considering the use of research impact to make decisions, this delay can become a significant and frustrating trait. Typically, by the time results from (especially larger) research projects have been analysed, interpreted and disseminated, policy has simply changed (e.g. due to a change of governance, economy or social climate). It can also take a considerable time for policy decisions to be approved (particularly at institutional or governmental levels). The effect of both delayed research impact and the possible subsequent lengthy policy approval process can severely affect how the research affects practice. Furthermore, when the results and subsequent impact of research indicate that policy decisions were incorrect, the impact of the research might be greater, but the findings may no longer be welcome and therefore disseminated. Other 'stumbling blocks' can include: lack of understanding of the research by policy-makers and research that is not 'in tune' with policy. Finally, changes in priorities for governing bodies, often coupled with rapid changes in legislation, can make long-term predictions of research impact problematic.

It is clear that the timing of research and the subsequent point at which impact will be assessed are critical decisions to make when considering policy and decision making. Research, by its very nature, takes time. This delay in outcomes needs to be fully considered when impact assessments are required to inform policy or decisions at all levels of organisations and governing bodies. Indeed, if quick decisions are required and there is sufficient baseline data, a retrospective approach is the best, but often not an ideally 'tailored' option for impact assessment.

Problems with the measurement of research impact

The multi-dimensional and transient nature of research make measuring research impact challenging. There have been very few attempts to measure the complexity and dynamics of research activities and how these affect not only their impact, but also the timing of when that impact will be observed or become apparent. We have little evidence to work on.

It can be challenging, for example, to understand the results of research and reflect on what 'impact' these results will have. This understanding requires both the consequence and the context of the research to be fully resolved and articulated; without this understanding the assessment of the impact is difficult. Additionally, all research can produce error or anomalies. Errors can severely affect one's confidence when assessing the impact of research data. A typical solution to address such concerns is to increase the amount of replication and subsequent data to garner greater statistical confidence. However, instead of producing clarity this can often lead to an increased level of difficultly in interpreting the data. Complex detail and a desire to be exact can stand in the way of understanding and thus implementation.

'Blue-skies' research

Most research that is considered to have potential impact is 'pure' or 'basic'; it is fundamental in nature and is designed to increase our understanding of various principles within subject disciplines. Although the immediate results of the research may not be immediately 'impactful' in terms of commercial or societal benefits, longer-term results can be. Indeed, they may lead to more applied research in the same subject area. Applied research typically utilises aspects of a 'mature' research community's theories, knowledge, methods, and techniques. It also typically leads to a defined outcome with significant local or wider impact (often driven by commercial or socio-economic concerns).

However, there is another type of research that contrasts with the above examples, generally known as 'blue skies' (typically, but not exclusively, scientific) research. 'Blue-skies' research usually takes place in domains where the 'real-world' applications are not immediately apparent or obvious. It has been defined as 'research without a clear goal' or purely 'curiosity-driven' research (see Braben, 2008). Supporters of blue-skies research argue that unanticipated research-based breakthroughs can be as valuable or of greater value than the outcomes of purely agenda-driven research. However, because of the inherently uncertain return on the initial investment into the research, blue-skies research is more difficult to 'pitch' (particularly in a funding context) as the impacts are more difficult to describe. As such, this type of research has increasingly become politically and commercially unpopular when compared to more applied research.

Nevertheless, in the context of when we might expect to see the impact of research one cannot simply ignore such research. In Reflection Point 5.4, some such research will undoubtedly have huge impacts upon governance and society, the timing of which is almost impossible to predict.

Unexpected research impact – the 'multiplier' effect

In recent years there have been more and more examples of collaborative and cross- (or multi-)disciplinary research. By working with more than one research group and by covering multiple areas of research activity it is possible not only to multiply the results of the research (which in themselves can have increased impact), but also to generate more examples of unexpected impact.

Indeed, in the context of research and researcher development within the UK, recent years have seen the Research Councils strongly encourage applications from teams for collaborative projects. More recently, the UK has seen the establishment of 'Doctoral Training Centres' (DTCs) and other similarly labelled centres of excellence, where universities within the UK are actively encouraged to collaborate on aspects of research and to provide a 'joined-up' approach to researcher development across disciplines. Some of the Research Councils within the UK are now insisting on this model of research collaboration and will only fund via a centre of excellence model. Any such centre of excellence pulls together researchers who are working on areas that address congruent elements of a research agenda with potential impact. The collaborating institutes draft joint operating agreements, submit joint funding proposals, with agreed outcomes and measures of impact. This is in complete contrast to the traditional mode of conducting research within a small section of one institution, guarding results against competitors; it is about joined-up thinking and collaboration as opposed to competition. The Research Councils specifically quote increased and sustainable impact as a key reason for establishing this mode of collaboration in future research activities within the UK (see RCUK, 2010a, 2010b).

When entering into ventures such as DTCs, it is important to consider the level of administrative support that this mode of collaboration requires. Once the collaboration is established and researchers recruited, they need to follow agreed protocols and share their results and conclusions. These are significant and 'game changing' considerations have to be given serious consideration, not least the amount of resource, including time, to be invested in establishing them. However, the heightened level of research activity and the increased opportunity for ideas and therefore potential subsequent impact is both enticing and palpable.

Measuring change in impact over time

The complexity of measuring impact over time

Within modern society there is a growing interest in the impacts of both academic and non-academic research. The past decade has seen a mounting desire to understand the spread, use and influence of research findings in both of these contexts. This is primarily related to current political imperatives to move beyond strictly academic interest to more practical (and typically, understandable) considerations of 'evidence', 'what works' and what has 'impact'; impact that clearly demonstrates a 'return on investment'.

These considerations are also no longer limited only to policy decisions, but increasingly as part of a wider public discourse. It is worth remembering that research-based evidence often has a relatively limited 'impact' upon on non-academic stakeholders who may not fully understand it. There is an increasing demand for greater public engagement and understanding for research to deliver in an impactful manner (see Chapters 7, 8 and 10). Greater focus is being placed on not only the directions of research enquiry but also the organisation of research, in an attempt to deliver greater impact with increased efficiency.

Those involved in research, as well as the funders or (potential) users of research, are increasingly aware of the limitations of simple (descriptive or prescriptive) models of research use and research impact. Further, the diversity of research, and the complexity of the means by which research findings may come into use, make understanding and assessing both academic and non-academic research impacts a challenging task.

With so many different stakeholders wanting so many different measures of impact it is easy to see that the dissemination of impact can be challenging, before even trying to understand when the timing of such impact should become apparent. It is important, therefore, that for prospective measurements of impact, both the audience and the data required to demonstrate impact are explicitly identified at the start of the project (Purcell et al., 2008).

How has the assessment of impact changed over time?

There are four main aspects when considering the historical measurements of impact that have occurred. They can be summarised as (i) instrumental, (ii) conceptual, (iii) academic and (iv) social (see Armstrong, 2011 for a more detailed explanation):

i. Instrumental assessments – are aimed at shaping legislation, policy development, aimed at altering behaviour.
ii. Conceptual assessments – are aimed at understanding how the impact of the research can affect policy.
iii. Academic measurements of impact – are usually highly demonstrable; they are made to advance either knowledge or policy, both within and across disciplines. The usual aim is to develop applications or theories.
iv. Social measurements – examine change, usually at the cultural or economic level. They are typically based on individual, organisational or national changes.

A rather obvious observation is that instrumental and conceptual measurements tend to be used to inform policy whereas academic and social measures of impact have been traditionally used to develop policy. It is important to remember, as has already been discussed, that these aspects of measurement can be somewhat limited or complicated by both the delay in which the impact of the research is seen, by the complexity of the research results or by a lack of baseline data.

Development of policy using academic and social measurements can inform decisions concerning the value of the areas being researched, hence, the impact. It is worth noting that value needs not simply to be related to financial or socio-economic concerns but can also address the development of researchers (see later in this chapter and Appendix I). This latter factor can be further informed by instrumental and conceptual assessments.

In recent years there has been a shift towards a much greater focus on the academic and social measurements of impact by researchers themselves (as opposed to funders of the research), as it is now common for funding applications to demand that these considerations are detailed in order for the award to be considered.

How to use the timing of impact to develop researchers

There are essentially four ways in which a focus on impact can be used to develop researchers (from Quinsee, 2011): (i) recognition (early) – collaborate with researchers and research students to celebrate and publicise the successes and impacts of their research, (ii) expertise (mid) – demonstrate research expertise through thought leadership, developing practice and/or research informed practice, (iii) development opportunities (established) – create and promote opportunities for researchers to engage with new research techniques and dialogue around their practice, which are informed by impact driven policy decisions and (iv) team (late) – exemplify good practice by actively participating in the sharing and development within institutions and beyond, both at regional and national levels.

It will be interesting, within the UK context, to see if there are tangible effects of investment in researcher development over the next few years. However, initiatives such as the IEG-IF (Bromley, 2009), the Researcher Concordat, the European Commission HR Excellence in Research Award and adherence to QAA recommendations (see Further reading for more details) suggest that we should see better developed and more confident researchers – both in the UK and beyond.

These initiatives are particularly timely as the competition to secure employment for emerging researchers is becoming increasingly challenging and the consideration of developmental impacts (both by the researcher and their managers) more important.

ACTIVITY 5.1   MEASURES OF IMPACT FOR THE FUTURE

It always useful to develop measures of impact for the future. As a guide, the following suggestions are worth considering: (i) What is the purpose of the research? (ii) What would others want to know about your research and its impact? (iii) What measures of impact are you currently using? (iv) Do these measures give you the information you need or do you need to collect other data?

Finally, if we are considering *when* we are to observe impact it is worth thinking about why you are looking for the impact and what purpose this impact will serve. The following key points should help to act as a checklist for such thoughts.

Key points

- Consider whether you have good baseline data for your impact assessment.
  - If yes – consider a retrospective assessment.
  - If no – look prospectively, but be clear about what you are attempting to measure, as well as the reasons for your measurement.
- Contemplate how long it will be before you see impact from your research, and what will affect this.
- Deliberate whether your research will deliver impact that is 'timely' for e.g. policy considerations.
- Remember that any impact measures can be unpredictable, particularly in large collaborations or in non-applied research.
- Weigh up how your measures of the impact of your research may change over time.
- There are good examples of measuring impact of individual researchers now available (see suggested reading list), which also consider the emergence of impact over time. Many of these measures are highly adaptable for considering the impacts from research activities in general.

Acknowledgements

The author would like to thank Dr Cathy Gibbons (University of Nottingham) and Ms Sarah Kearns (Plymouth University) for useful discussions and comments on the draft manuscript.

Further reading

1994 Group (2009) Impact of Roberts Funding at 1994 Group Institutions, Research Report http://www2.le.ac.uk/departments/gradschool/about/external/publications/roberts-impact.pdf (accessed 26 April 2013).

Armstrong, Fiona (2011) 'The impact journey'. Available at: http://www.methods.manchester.ac.uk/impact/seminar-6/Armstrong.pdf

Aspinwall, K., Simkins, T., Wilkinson, J.F. and McAuley, M. J. (1992) *Managing Evaluation in Education: A Developmental Approach*, London: Routledge.

Braben, D.W. (2008) *Scientific Freedom: The Elixir of Civilization*. Chichester: John Wiley and Sons.

Bromley, T. (2009) The Rugby Team Impact Framework: One Year On, Cambridge: Careers Research Advisory Centre (CRAC). Available at: www.vitae.ac.uk/impact

Bromley, T. (2010) The Impact of Researcher Training and Development: Two Years on, Cambridge: Careers Research Advisory Centre (CRAC). Available at: www.vitae.ac.uk/impact

Bromley, T., Metcalf, J. and Park, C. (2008) *The Rugby Team Impact Framework*. Available at: www.vitae.ac.uk/impact

Concordat to Support the Career Development of Researchers: an agreement between the funders and employers of researchers in the UK. Available at: http://www.vitae.ac.uk/concordat

Goldfarb, S. (2011) 'The greater impact of the LHC: what's in it for the rest of the world?' Available at: http://ippog.web.cern.ch/sites/ippog.web.cern.ch/files/import/goldfarbimpactpaper.pdf

Kearns, P. and Miller, T. (1997) *Measuring the Impact of Training and Development on the Bottom Line*, London: Pitman.

Kirkpatrick, D.L. and Kirkpatrick, J.D. (2006) *Evaluating Training Programmes*, 3rd edition, San Francisco: Berrett-Koehler.

McGlynn, E.A., Asch, S.M., Adams, J., Keesey, J., Hicks, J., DeCristofaro, A. and Kerr, E.A. (2003) 'The quality of health care delivered to adults in the United States', *New England Journal of Medicine*, 348: 2635–45.

Quality Assurance Agency (2004) Code of practice for the assurance of academic quality and standards in higher education. *Section 1: Postgraduate Research Programmes*.

Quality Assurance Agency (2007) Report on the review of research degree programmes: England and Northern Ireland.

Purcell, K., Elias, P. and Tzanakou, C. (2008) Doctoral Careers Pathway Study, Skills and Training: options analysis for the collection of information about the early careers of UK doctoral graduates. Warwick Institute for Employment Research. Available at: http://www.rcuk.ac.uk/documents/researchcareers/opana.pdf

Quinsee, S. (2011) 'Turning coffee drinking into key performance indicators: creating meaningful educational development measures', *Educational Developments*, 12 (2): 1–5.

RCUK (2009) Roberts Report's summary. Research Councils UK. Available at: http://www.rcuk.ac.uk/documents/researchcareers/08repsum.pdf (accessed 26 April 2013).

RCUK (2009) Research Careers and Diversity Strategy. Research Councils UK. Available at: www.rcuk.ac.uk/rescareer/strategy.htm (accessed 26 April 2013).

RCUK (2010a) Review of the progress in implementing the recommendations of Sir Gareth Roberts, regarding employability and career development of PhD students and research staff, Research Councils UK. Available at: http://www.rcuk.ac.uk./documents/researchcareers/IndependentReviewHodge.pdf (accessed 26 June 2013).

RCUK (2010b) Analysis of HEI Roberts Reports 2004 and 2009 for the Roberts Skills Panel, Research Councils UK http://www.rcuk.ac.uk/documents/researchcareers/IndependentReviewHodge.pdf (accessed 26 April 2013).

Roberts, G. (2001) 'SET for success'. Available at: http://webarchive.nationalarchives.gov.uk/+/http:/www.hm-treasury.gov.uk/set_for_success.htm

Saunders, M. (2000) 'Beginning an evaluation with RUFDATA: theorizing a practical approach to evaluation planning', *Evaluation*, 6 (1) 7–21.

Vitae (2005, 2006, 2007, 2008, 2009 and 2010) Database of practice. Available at: www.vitae.ac.uk/dop

Vitae (2006) *Evaluation of Skills Development of Early Career Researchers – a Strategy Paper from the Rugby Team*. Available at: www.vitae.ac.uk/cms/files/Rugby-Team-annual-report-January-2006.pdf

Vitae Researcher Development Conference (2008). Available at:www.vitae.ac.uk/policy-practice/13491/Vitae-Researcher-Development-Conference-2008.html

Vitae Researcher Development Framework (2010). Available at: www.vitae.ac.uk/rdf

Warry, P. (2006) 'Increasing the economic impact of Research Councils'. Available at: http://www.vitae.ac.uk/policy-practice/1682/Government-reviews-and-reports.html

Wisker, G. (2006) 'Educational developments – how do we know it's working? How do we know how well we are doing?' *Educational Developments* 7 (3): 11–1.

6

HOW CAN IMPACT BE PLANNED INTO RESEARCH PROPOSALS?

ROB DALEY AND SARA SHINTON

Key points

- The role of impact in a research proposal
- Sections in a proposal that deal with impact
- How impact is evaluated within the peer review process
- Identifying probable impacts
- Costing impact related activities
- Support available to researchers from institutional sources.

The role of impact in a research proposal

Although the Impact Agenda is a relatively new development in academia, the wider notion of research impact has long been embedded in funding proposals. Researchers have always been called upon to articulate the potential benefits and implications of their work. Research conducted in the academic environment has always been disseminated, considered and utilised in a range of ways by other users. Many funding bodies have played a role in this, working with partners in the commercial, governmental, health and third sectors to ensure the research they fund has the greatest possible consequences.

Rebecca Steliaros, EPSRC's former senior impact and evaluation manager and now an independent impact consultant, says that –

> the Government and Research Councils want to see research projects making a positive impact on the world just as much as the researchers themselves. Ensuring that researchers plan to maximise their impact and integrating these ideas into proposals from an early stage is vital for success. Once a project is running, pro-active management to maximise impact throughout a project is essential. Impact should not be thought of as a 'bolt-on' but integrated with what a successful research leader does. Impact is here to stay and will become ever more important as the UK faces the future in an increasingly competitive, globalised world.

The key change in recent years has been to facilitate the connection between researcher and potential user. For this to be done effectively, researchers need to consider these wider beneficiaries from the start of the research cycle (as described in Chapters 2 and 4). Many funding bodies appreciate that developing relationships with new partners will take time and require investment which should be considered as a twist to the title of this chapter – *the role of research proposals in impact* is key, as funding can be provided to support any activities which will help to achieve any identified benefits.

The structure of proposals varies with individual funders, but at the heart of all the processes we have considered are a number of features of effective impact activities:

- Embedded – the impact related activities are integral to the research project, not just 'bolted on' at the dissemination stage.
- Project specific – as most funding is provided for projects, the impact activities must relate to the work being funded (this can be more general for personal fellowships and awards) and should not describe activities which relate to previous work or wider university responsibilities. Evidence of a strong track record in wider engagement is useful, but the focus should be on the research for which funding is sought.
- Relationships – in order to achieve an embedded strategy and facilitate a process of producing outputs which are usable by other partners, there should be evidence of a developing relationship between researchers and stakeholders. The involvement of beneficiaries from the outset builds such feasibility into the proposal.
- Commitment – the proposal should reflect commitment to both academic and non-academic impact, even if the former is the natural outcome of the research. There should be focus on knowledge exchange and impact (see Chapter 10), rather than simple dissemination.

In considering your own impact strategy in a research proposal, these translate into a series of questions:

- How has my awareness of the needs of wider stakeholders helped me to develop my proposed research ideas?
- What value do the outputs of this project have to other partners?
- What support do I need to achieve the potential impact of this work?

As the next section will outline, different funders have different approaches to impact in proposals. In some cases the ways in which impact will be achieved must be carefully outlined. On others, the potential benefits must be described, but without details on how these will come about.

What do proposal forms require? (What boxes must be completed?)

A consistent call for research with impact is evident in the application forms of all major funding providers. However, each funding provider has its own process which reflects its funding strategy and vision. The definitions of impact also vary, providing researchers with a choice of funding streams and the opportunity to find a funding partner who will value your approach to achieving impact.

Research Councils – all of the UK Research Councils share an impact strategy and, alongside HEFCE through the REF criteria, have been the main drivers of the Impact Agenda. All Research Council funding applications now include an impact summary and 'Pathways to Impact' section. The Research Councils often publish the impact summaries of projects that they fund on their website. It is important that you do not include any confidential information in this section.

The impact summary should identify all the potential benefits if the research is successful and produces the expected outcomes. These include academic, societal and economic as appropriate to the research. The impact summary should answer two questions:

1. Who will benefit from this research?
2. How will they benefit from this research? (I.e. what value and relevance this research has for them)

The 'Pathways to Impact' section describes *how* the benefits described in the impact summary will be achieved. Although it is intended to focus on partners and beneficiaries beyond academia, if wider academic engagement is essential to achieving broader economic and social benefits, this can be included. This section should answer the question:

- What will be done to ensure that potential beneficiaries have the opportunity to engage with this research?

The Research Councils have produced extensive supporting material on their website to help researchers understand the purpose of the impact questions and to support the development of impact strategies. At the time of writing these include an impact toolkit on the ESRC website (ESRC, no date) and a series of videos describing impact on the EPSRC website (ESP-SRC, no date). Both the NERC (NERC, no date) and the BBSRC (BBSRC, no date) provide guidance on the scoring on impact statements on their websites. These resources will continue to be developed and extended as the pool of successful impact initiatives grows. Although they will always reflect the Research Councils' concept of impact, these resources offer advice and examples to researchers across the board of disciplines.

Other funding providers tend not to have a specific impact section, putting the onus on the researcher to embed their impact strategy in the project description. Some examples are summarised next.

Joseph Rowntree Foundation (JRF) – with a focus on social justice and a commitment to a more equal society, it is unsurprising that the impact sought from research funded by JRF is to influence policy and practice. Their application form asks researchers to outline the '**policy and practice relevance**' of their work.

The Leverhulme Trust – looks to fund research which is creative, risky and spans traditional discipline boundaries. Although impact is not referred to explicitly, one of their research criteria is 'the extent to which the outcomes of the research can contribute to wider **cultural well-being**' and they look at 'the opportunity provided by the proposed research for the **personal development** of those involved'.

Wellcome Trust – impact features at the heart of their funding strategy although, again, it is not mentioned explicitly. The three areas of funding focus are supporting outstanding researchers, accelerating the application of research and exploring medicine in historical and cultural contexts.

The Royal Society – the potential benefits of research are outlined in the lay summary section on their application forms:

> Please provide a lay summary of your proposed project. This should be understandable to an A-level science student. You should explain why you have chosen to work in this subject area and what it is about your proposed research that you find particularly exciting, interesting or important. Please also explain the potential impact or wider benefits to society of your research.

The third (charity) sector is another significant funder of research. At *Cancer Research UK (CRUK)*, as with other charities, the benefits of proposed research must be apparent and relevant in the research question and the project's core aims. Their funding applications include the section

'Purpose', which looks for evidence of future impact beyond knowledge generation:

> State briefly the objectives of the proposed research and the significance of the results that may be obtained (e.g. eventual clinical application, impact on policy and practice) and their relevance to cancer.

Joanna Reynolds, the Director of Centres, Operations and Reporting for Cancer Research UK, explains why the impact of research is so important in the charity sector.

> Cancer Research UK is an organisation that relies entirely on the generosity of its donors, so evaluating and articulating the impact of the research we fund has always been important for us. But in a more challenging economic climate and with increasing scrutiny of public funding, our needs and expectations have increased. We ask all applicants for funding to explain the potential impact of their work on cancer and this is an important part of the funding decision. Recipients of CRUK funding are expected to participate in public engagement activities and – particularly for translational and clinical research – on-going funding may be contingent on reaching milestones. As results emerge, it is essential that we are able to capture, understand and articulate the impact of the research both to ensure that it reaches its potential and to secure and guide future funding.

While much of this chapter focuses on impact outside academia, you should ensure that you give appropriate consideration to the academic impact of your research within your proposal. Research Council applications require all applicants to complete a section on the academic benefits of their project. This should identify the specific contribution that your research will make to knowledge within the UK and internationally. You should also identify how your research will benefit both researchers within your own subject area and those researchers in other disciplines.

The MRC have a long history of funding research with wider benefits and have collected for years feedback from their researchers about the nature of these benefits. Ian Viney, MRC Head of Strategic Evaluation, explains:

> For more than 15 years grant applications for MRC funding have included a section on 'health and wealth benefits', which encouraged researchers to ensure potential beneficiaries were included in communications and where appropriate research design and potential impacts were outlined from the start. The other distinguishing aspect to MRC's approach was the implementation of MRC e-Val (now 'Researchfish') as a structured and comprehensive

way to collect feedback from researchers about, inter alia, progress and productivity, taking a holistic view of output which covers ways in which researchers influence policy, communicate their research and develop new products.

As expertise and understanding of impact develops in the sector, resources will continue to be added to the websites of the major funding bodies to support researchers developing their own approaches.

In addition to the impact elements already discussed, fellowship applications may also include a section on the expected impact of the fellowship on your development as a researcher and research leader. This is an important element of fellowship applications and should be given due consideration when developing your proposal (see Chapters 9 and 11 for further information for self-development). Many universities provide tailored support and advice to fellowship applicants through their research office or their staff development function.

In summary, the Research Councils are unusual in the explicit way they require impact to be addressed but, in demanding from researchers details of how they propose to achieve impact and in offering funding to support these activities, they are acknowledging the additional efforts that researchers must make to establish effective impact strategies. Other funding bodies have different attitudes about the extent to which they expect researchers to engage with external partners, but they are consistent in wanting their research to make a difference and to be available to those who could take it further.

How do referees evaluate impact plans?

The funders' guidance for referees normally asks them to comment on:

- How realistic the identified impacts are
- The effectiveness of the intended activities

The Research Councils are the only funding body currently evaluating impact plans. Other funding bodies require information on impact, but do not explicitly ask for details about how this will be realised. The evaluation of impact plans is done as part of the proposal review and the feedback on plans contributes to the decision-making process. Despite concerns from some circles, the Research Councils have stated clearly that their principal criteria for funding remains excellence and that an outstanding piece of research would not be rejected because of a poor impact strategy. However, their commitment to stronger impact comes from a belief that it will lead to better research (see also Chapter 2). Thinking about impact and thinking about potential beneficiaries of research at an early stage gives a researcher a different perspective on their work and could lead to stronger outputs. The purpose of Pathways to Impact is to integrate this thinking into the application process.

Reviewers are asked to consider how effective and realistic the applicants have been in identifying the potential impacts of their research (impact summary), and then to relate these to the range and appropriateness of activities that the researcher is planning to achieve these impacts (the Pathways to Impact section). This second element is of particular interest to the reviewer and, from their reactions to proposals presented so far, it is possible to draw out questions which reflect their approach to evaluation (presented as Box 6.1).

BOX 6.1   EVALUATION QUESTIONS A REVIEWER MIGHT HAVE IN MIND

- Do the proposed activities to achieve impact actually relate to the outcomes?
- Will they enable the researchers to achieve their impact objectives?
- Are these activities integrated throughout the broader project?
- Are opportunities for impact identified and exploited throughout the lifetime of the grant?
- Are the proposed impact activities a good fit for the research and will they support significant impact?
- Are end-users likely to be engaged by the means suggested?
- Has the management of impact activities been well thought out?
- Are the objectives for the Pathways to Impact clear, achievable and realistic?

Although impact is a secondary criterion, it is an important aspect that will be considered at the panel stage. If two equally excellent proposals are presented, the quality of the Pathways to Impact statement will form part of the decision-making process to award funding. The Research Councils' commitment to impact is such that they reserve the right to delay funding whilst they support researchers in developing more effective impact strategies. A member of a recent EPSRC panel has confirmed that:

> At panel meetings, Impact can play an important role when deciding the relative strengths between two proposals of comparable scientific merit.

Identifying your possible and probable impacts (What? How? Who?)

The process of writing impact into a grant proposal starts long before the deadline. Impact requires the development of relationships and understanding of other partners, which will take time to establish. This section will look at the key questions that must be answered in proposals and offers suggestions which you can relate to your own research. These questions come from the Research Councils' application process so you should refer to the guidance from your own funding body to ensure this framework will apply to their needs.

What does impact look like?

As defined by the Research Councils, a broad range of potential outcomes of research fall under the Impact Agenda as shown in the diagram entitled 'The Pathways to Impact framework provided by RCUK', which can be found in Appendix III. As case studies emerge, these definitions may develop – it is always important to be aware of the latest guidance from the Research Council and other funders and regulators as you shape your strategy.

This list of potential impacts has been written to cover all the various disciplines and research topics funded by Research Councils in the UK so as an individual researcher you should look for the impacts that are most consistent with your own interests and approach. Concerns about the timescales over which impact has to present itself are often misplaced – impact does not mean early exploitation. Funders understand that impact from research takes time, often 15 to 20 years to occur, and that impacts will appear at different stages of a project. Chapter 5 elaborates on this. These timescales are not always consistent with their funding streams, which are usually on much shorter timescales. None of these factors should deter you. Impact will and should be generated through diverse pathways involving different patterns and approaches. The evaluation of impact plans will be in the context of research and will be done by people who are familiar with the research process and its challenges.

REFLECTION POINT 〰〰

Consider what kinds of impact your research might make, using the diagram in Appendix III.

Who might benefit from your research?

The range of stakeholders who are affected by, interested in or able to apply research from universities is as diverse as the research itself. In order to identify the stakeholders who could form part of your impact strategy, you need to think in general terms about what your research might lead to, what difference it might make in the immediate and longer term and whose interests it overlaps with. A mind map is a useful tool and it might help to develop this with colleagues, particularly those from other disciplines (as this will help you to broaden your thinking). Mind maps (Buzan, 2009) and their use in evaluation are covered in Chapter 8.

As part of its impact toolkit, the ESRC has developed a list of potential stakeholders which might help you to identify those which tie in with your research interests. Table 6.1 contains a brief list of different stakeholder types grouped by their closeness/distance from the research activity.

TABLE 6.1 Potential stakeholders who may help to effect the impact of your research

	Stakeholder identity
Close to you and your project	• Academics, PhD students, administrative and communications staff • Universities, institutes, independent research organisations • Academic networks – academic groups, centres and institutes including learned societies, subject networks • Industrial partners with common interests – pharmaceutical, manufacturing, finance, construction industries (as examples) • Small and medium-sized enterprises
Looking more widely	• Clinicians and patient groups • Other research funders i.e. Research Councils, Technology Strategy Board, Joseph Rowntree Foundation, Wellcome Trust • Policy – national and regional assemblies, government departments, civil servants, local government
Looking beyond research communities	• Practitioners – professional bodies i.e. Chartered Management Institute, business, trade unions, third sector, charities, voluntary organisations and social enterprises • General public – local community groups, local business groups, pressure groups • Media – local paper, radio, TV station, national correspondents, national programmes • International media, online, trade and specialist publications

REFLECTION POINT

Can you identify your potential partners and beneficiaries?

How will they benefit from this research?

Once you have started to identify potential partners for your impact strategy, you need to think about the value that your research will have for them. The most effective way to determine this is to talk to them! Many funding bodies talk about 'partners' in their impact strategies and there is an expectation that the approaches of individual researchers will be partnerships with stakeholders rather than a 'jug to mug' model where the outcomes of research are presented without consultation or involvement.

At this stage of your thinking, you need to keep considering the bigger picture and how you will ultimately explain how your proposed research has the potential to contribute to the nation's health, wealth or culture. The involvement of your stakeholders is likely to be critical to this, so it is important to listen to their views on how your research outputs need to be framed to reach and influence the right people.

REFLECTION POINT

Think about what steps you will need to take between now and the start of the project to ensure potential beneficiaries are involved in the right ways.

What will you do to realise the impacts?

This final critical question must be explicitly answered for Research Council applications, although it is also integral to other proposals. One important consideration here is not just what you are going to do, but also when you are going to do it, as well as how often you are going to do it. It is important that when you are planning your interactions with stakeholders that these are building on-going relationships so that they lead to regular interaction rather than one-off activities. Activity 6.1, engaging with stakeholders who may help to maximise the impact of your research, contains some useful prompts to consider as you plan your activities to effect impact for your project.

In order to avoid impact statements which rely solely on academic mechanisms such as conferences, publications and workshops, the funding bodies are building up a bank of case studies and good practice to showcase how impact can be achieved (NERC, no date; EPSRC, no date; ESRC, no date; RCUK, 2010a, 2010b). They are keen for this good practice to be emulated and developed, so a sensible starting point for any impact strategy should be to read the case studies as they emerge.

ACTIVITY 6.1   ENGAGING WITH STAKEHOLDERS WHO MAY HELP TO MAXIMISE THE IMPACT OF YOUR RESEARCH

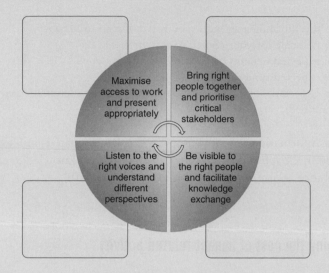

Plan your communication and engagement strategy to ensure impact is planned into your research process. Write the communication and dissemination channels in the boxes associated with each objective. These could include: conferences, workshops, websites, newsletters, social media, inviting visitors into your research environment, visiting other partners, staff secondments.

What can you do to effect impact and how do you present this in a proposal?

There are a number of different approaches to ensuring that your research has impact. The choice of approach will depend on the nature of your research and the expertise and experience of the research team. Most approaches commonly used by researchers fall into five broad categories:

1. knowledge exchange with commercial organisations;
2. knowledge exchange with policy-makers;
3. public engagement with specific audiences;
4. public engagement through the media;
5. co-creation of knowledge.

When writing your proposal it is important to identify what approaches and activities you (and your co-researchers) are planning to undertake to maximise the impact of your research. You should try to provide as much information as possible regarding:

- the specific audiences with whom you intend to engage;
- the rationale for your choice of activities;
- the expected benefits of these engagements;
- the expected timescales of these benefits;
- the expected outcomes and how these may be identified (and if possible, quantified).

(Further information on how impact can be evaluated and evidenced is presented in Chapters 7 and 8 while elaboration on knowledge exchange as a contributor to impact can be found in Chapter 10.)

Identifying the cost of impact-related activity

Having identified what the likely impact activity for your project is, it is vital that you consider the resources that you will require to effect that impact. Assuming that your funder will allow you to build such funding into your project, you should provide sensible plans with associated costs. If your funder will not fund this aspect of the project then you should consider other sources of such funding and provide an overview of this and how you intend to access them in your proposal. These costs will vary greatly depending on the impact activities that you are planning. Costs for the following may be incurred:

- printing publications for non-academic audiences;
- dissemination events, including your travel costs, subsistence, accommodation if necessary, etc.;
- development of websites and other multi-media products, videos etc.;
- people time to manage and deliver the above activities;
- people exchange costs (secondments, exchange visits, etc.);
- business development costs.

If your proposed impact plans include collaboration or cooperation with other organisations, it is important to consider their costs and any contributions they could/will make to these activities. This may be in terms of cash to support impact-related activities or may be 'in-kind' contributions/support. Your proposal should try to capture the full costs of these activities as this will demonstrate to reviewers that you have given thorough consideration to maximising the impact of the proposed research[1] as well as increasing the overall value of the proposed project when compared to the support requested from the funders. Evidence of such co-operation/collaboration as well as evidence of cash and in-kind contributions should be included with your proposal. These are usually in the form of letters of support outlining the different contributions that other organisations will make to the project. It is worth noting that, while any letter of support is better than none, the quality of these letters is given due consideration by referees and by award panels. It is important that, when you organise letters of support, the letters should contain a convincing case clearly identifying the importance of this project to the organisation, the extent of their contribution to the project and the usefulness of the expected outcomes to them.

Post-project plans to effect, identify and evaluate impact

One element often ignored in research proposals is planning for post-project activity. From a funder's perspective, the funding for the project is given not just to see the project completed successfully, but for the longer-term benefits that the project will bring about. Many of these benefits will occur after the funded project is completed and the activities that are required by the researcher to maximise these benefits are unlikely to be eligible for funding through the project. However, researchers should highlight what activities they intend to carry out post-project to maximise the impact of the research and, where appropriate, to identify how they will fund these activities. This may be through future funding proposals, through applying for follow-on funding or knowledge transfer partnership (KTP) type funding, or through activities that require little direct cash funding (e.g. maintaining a website, continued user engagement, etc.).

One important post-project activity is the evaluation of the impact of the research and further details of this are included in Chapters 7 and 8.

The responsibilities of institutions

As impact becomes a more important aspect of research, the support provided by research organisations and institutions for researchers around impact has grown. Most institutions have units with a research support function,

---

[1]Extensive information on the costing of project proposals can be found in another book in the series: *Success in Research: Developing Research Proposals.*

which now include staff who can provide advice on how to strengthen the Pathways to Impact statements in research proposals. Most organisations also have specialist staff to advise on effecting impact through collaboration with industry and commercial organisations – see also Chapter 10. Some of the larger institutions have specialist staff to support researchers in effecting impact through policy and through collaboration with non-commercial organisations, with some of these units being focused on specialist research or policy areas. Most universities offer staff development support in writing research proposals and understanding and effecting impact. This is commonly through workshop programmes but may also be through mentoring and coaching provided by experienced academic staff or by specialists in that area. The research support function within your faculty or university should also be able to help you to identify the appropriate costs of impact-related activities. The University of Leeds has estimated some of these costs (University of Leeds, 2012) and these may guide your own deliberations.

As a researcher, it is important that you gain a good understanding of the support that your institution offers and that you know how to use this to best effect when preparing your proposals. All researchers are advised to contact the relevant people within their organisation to identify the support available. Discussions with experienced researchers are also encouraged to ensure that all possible means of support are identified at the outset of the proposal writing and project planning.

As one example of how an academic plans and manages their engagement activities, a short case study, in the form of an interview, is presented here.

CASE STUDY 6.1   ENGAGEMENT ACTIVITIES

Dr Peter Matthews
Peter is a lecturer at the School of the Built Environment, Heriot-Watt University. His research focuses on issues of spatial inequality, community engagement, public service performance, and regeneration and renewal. The following is a summary of an interview with Peter about his engagement activities.

How do you identify the audiences that you to engage with?

I try to identify who would be interested in the research. Those I expect to be interested in my research include policy-makers, community groups and community members. There are also the unexpected audiences; one of my reports was downloaded by a government agency in Australia while a report that I authored for the Equalities and Human

Rights Commission Scotland (EHRC) was reported in a number of newspapers including the *Scottish Sun*!

How do you choose your engagement activities?

I try to be pro-active with my engagement activities. I design and run specific workshops to inform and to engage various audiences in my research. I also write articles for professional publications to try to reach specific professional audiences. However, I am also open to new opportunities and will react to any offers to engage with different groups. I was recently invited to present to a Scottish Parliament cross-party group on health inequalities.

What are the benefits of these activities?

The benefits of my engagement are very varied. All engagement activities help to broaden and improve my professional profile and help to widen my network. They allow me to gain a better understanding of the challenges that are faced by less advantaged communities and by policy-makers. They also allow me to be a participant in the social debate around the issues that my research is concerned with. I much prefer to be a participant rather than an observer from the outside. Being an 'unreconstructed social democrat' and activist-academic I hope that these allow me to help make the world a better place.

What are the timescales for these benefits?

My present projects, for example in a local deprived neighbourhood, deliver some initial impact such as carving and raising a digital 'totem pole' in some green space. However, the more important impacts are the longer-term ones such as sustainability, 'Will the community be sustained over the next few years?' and 'What benefits will that bring to the community members?' These activities also provide longer-term learning about community engagement. This is of benefit to me and the rest of the team and some of this learning will be shared with other researchers to help inform their engagement activities. My engagement activities also present me with new ways of viewing the issues and challenges faced by community members and policy-makers and help to bring about new research questions, which, in time, will hopefully lead to new research projects and further engagement activities.

Final checklist

Once you have completed your proposal and have checked it against the guidance provided by the funder, you should ask yourself the following final questions, presented in Box 6.2.

BOX 6.2   FINAL CHECKLIST QUESTIONS BEFORE SUBMITTING THE PROPOSAL

1. Have all appropriate partners and end-users been identified in the proposal?
2. Has evidence been provided about how these end-users have contributed to the proposal development?
3. Have you demonstrated a clear understanding of how your research meets specific end-user needs?
4. Do the letters of support that accompany your proposal demonstrate their commitment to the project and their confidence that the project will deliver real impact?
5. Are all the proposed impact-related activities appropriate for the project and is their management suitably considered?
6. Are the impact related resources that have been requested appropriate for the activities proposed?

Acknowledgements

The authors would like to thank all those who contributed quotes for this chapter and Dr Peter Matthews for contributing the case study. The authors also acknowledge the contribution of Janet Wilkinson of Three Times Three Consulting for her role in shaping the chapter's structure and content.

Further reading

As previously mentioned, it is important that all researchers keep up to date with the guidance from funders and on how impact will be considered in any research evaluation exercises. The researcher should also keep up to date with guidance from their own organisation. The following resources will be of interest to researchers who wish to understand further how they might plan and effect impact through engagement activities and should help you to present these in research proposals.

1. *Maximising the Impact of Your Research: A Handbook for Social Scientists*, compiled by the LSE Public Policy Group and available online at http://www2. lse.ac.uk/government/research/resgroups/LSEPublicPolicy/Docs/LSE_ Impact_Handbook_April_2011.pdf (accessed 2 November 2012).
2. *The KT and Impact Health Check, A Self-assessment Guide to Benchmarking and Planning your Research Impact Engagement Activities*, produced by the Issues

Project and available at http://www.urbansustainabilityexchange.org.uk/media/ISSUES%20Outputs/Health%20Check/HealthCheck_bookletv1.pdf (accessed on 2 November 2012).

3. *Introduction to Knowledge Exchange, A Set of Guidance Materials for Researchers*, produced by the Issues Project and available at http://www.urbansustainability exchange.org.uk/media/Guidance%20Notes%20Set.pdf (accessed on 2 November 2012).

4. *Social Media: A Guide for Researchers*, produced by the International Centre for Guidance Studies for the Research Information Network. This guide provides researchers with guidance on how different social media tools can be used in research and in engagement and impact activities. It is available at http://www.rin.ac.uk/our-work/communicating-and-disseminating-research/social-media-guide-researchers (accessed on 2 November 2012).

References

BBSRC (no date) 'Pathways to Impact scoring criteria'. Available at http://www.bbsrc.ac.uk/funding/apply/impact/pathways-to-impact.aspx (accessed 6 August 2012).

Buzan, T. (2009) *The Mind Map Book*, London: Pearson Publications.

EPSRC (no date) 'Economic and social impact case studies'. Available at: http://www.epsrc.ac.uk/newsevents/pubs/corporate/annualreport/annualreport0910/economicimpact/casestudies/Pages/default.aspx (accessed 3 August 2012).

ESRC (no date) 'Impact case studies'. Available at: http://www.esrc.ac.uk/impacts-and-findings/features-casestudies/case-studies/index.aspx (accessed 3 August 2012).

ESRC (no date) 'Impact tool kit'. Available at: http://www.esrc.ac.uk/funding-and-guidance/tools-and-resources/impact-toolkit/index.aspx (accessed 6 August 2012).

NERC (no date) 'Pathways to Impact frequently asked questions'. Available at: http://www.nerc.ac.uk/funding/application/documents/faqs.pdf (accessed 6 August 2012).

NERC (no date) 'Science impact database'. Available at: http://sid.nerc.ac.uk/ (accessed 3 August 2012).

RCUK (2010a) 'Pathways to Impact'. Available at: http://www.rcuk.ac.uk/documents/impacts/RCUKtypologydiagram.pdf (accessed 3 August 2012).

RCUK (2010b) 'Pathways to Impact case studies'. Available at: http://www.rcuk.ac.uk/media/brief/impactcase/Pages/home.aspx (accessed 12 December 2012).

University of Leeds (2012) 'Impact guidance'. Available at: www.engineering.leeds.ac.uk/researchfinance/info/documents/ImpactGuidanceEngineeringJune11.docx (accessed 3 August 2012).

7

HOW CAN IMPACT EVALUATION BE PLANNED?

TONY BROMLEY AND ANDRÉ DE CAMPOS

Key points

- Impact evaluation planning
- The use of the Realistic Evaluation approach as an underpinning principle for impact evaluation
- The relationship between impact evaluation planning and methodological choice
- Strategic considerations when selecting an object for evaluation
- How to conceive a logic diagram to support the impact evaluation
- How to plan the implementation of the evaluation and to reflect on its results

Underpinning principles: realistic evaluation

The approach for planning the evaluation of impact described in this chapter draws upon themes from a number of approaches. On the practical side, the main ones are project management and the development of tool kits (Buttrick, 2009; Turner, 2002; de Campos, 2010a) and on the conceptual side the societal impacts of publicly funded academic research (Warry, 2006; ESRC, 2009; de Campos, 2010b). However, the key underpinning principle considered here is that of Realistic Evaluation discussed below (Pawson and Tilley, 1997).

Another key theme is that impact evaluation planning should be embedded from the start in the planning and design of any proposed 'activity'.[1] If the issue that needs to be addressed by the activity is clearly identified, then the evaluation can be planned to assess to what extent the identified issue has been addressed by outcomes from the activity. Therefore, the evaluation should be designed to determine whether the outcomes from the activity did realise the impact required to address the initially identified issue. The evaluation then becomes logical and clear.

Logically working through a proposed evaluation in this way before starting an activity will mean that any activity can be better designed and the expected impact can be defined in a clearer fashion. As will be discussed below, the evaluation must be guided by a strategy, which should also been seen as something that can undergo some change as more is understood and an activity is implemented. This is conceptually akin to project management. No project management plan remains completely unchanged from the moment it is first created to the completion of the project.

In relation to the underpinning principle, Figure 7.1 shows a representation of Realistic Evaluation.

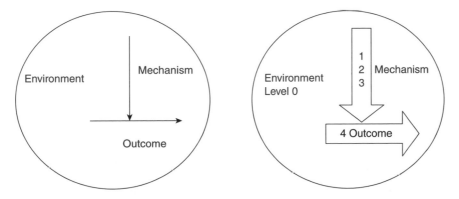

FIGURE 7.1   A representation of a realistic evaluation

The first oval provides a schematic representation of realistic evaluation. A mechanism operates in an environment which leads to an outcome. The second figure expresses a logic diagram for realising impact for a research project in realistic evaluation terms. See Table 7.1 for an explanation of the numbered steps for an illustrative research project logic diagram or Figure 7.5 for a learning logic diagram.
(Source T. Bromley and J. Metcalfe (2012) after Pawson and Tilley (1997) and Kirkpatrick and Kirkpatrick (2006))

A Mechanism operates in an Environment[2] and leads to an Outcome. So what does this mean? If we consider Environment first, this characterises the conditions in which we are operating. We might consider the contextual conditions that influence economic, social, policy, professional practice or

---

[1]The word 'activity' is used here in a broad sense. To reflect your specific context 'activity' might be replaced by 'research project', 'project' or even 'intervention'. The choice of word here won't alter the evaluation methodology.
[2]In Pawson and Tilley (1997) the word 'context' is used rather than the word 'environment' which is an adaptation for this application of realistic evaluation ideas.

cultural impacts and/or the attitude and behaviours of people (Warry, 2006). For example, an environment of an education programme that is well resourced, with positive, inspirational staff working in state-of-the-art facilities differs considerably from an environment of lack of resources, staff with low motivation levels and out-of-date facilities. If the same initiative (or 'activity') is attempted in each of these environments, it is likely that each will exert different types of influence on the activity. Therefore the outcomes and impact of the activity itself will be different. It is important to understand the environment before any initiative takes place (baseline environment).

Understanding the baseline environment should include: considering what is currently in place (for instance in the education example: programme structure, number of courses, number of staff, communication systems, etc.); understanding the needs of stakeholders and drivers for change; and understanding the factors external to the proposed activity that may influence the realisation of the expected outcomes and related impacts. This also entails understanding attribution in relation to the contribution of the particular activity to the outcomes and impacts identified (these ideas are developed further in Chapter 8).

Once the baseline environment is understood the inputs needed in order to realise the desired outcomes and impact can be considered along with a logical consideration of how the changes will achieve the outcomes and impact. This can result in a logic diagram discussed below.

A further supportive concept in understanding impact, and the attribution of any activity to achieving an impact, is to consider the expected outcomes and related impacts of an activity in terms of the time after an activity starts when an impact will become apparent against the number of potential contributory factors to the impact being realised. Figures 7.2 (academic impacts) and 7.3 (social impacts) illustrate this point by mapping the statements of potential impacts of research highlighted by the UK Research Councils in their 'Pathways to Impact'.[3]

The mapping is constructed by considering each statement of the potential impact of research put forward by RCUK, positioning the statement on the diagram appropriately to reflect the balance of how many potential contributory factors there are to the realisation of the impact (vertical axis) and how long after the start of the research project the impact is likely to be realised (horizontal axis).

Figure 7.4 shows an evaluation flow chart that expresses the key elements of the methodology outlined above as a step-by-step process. Table 7.1 illustrates how the flow chart can be used to generate an evaluation map (for further details, see 'Key elements for a study' later in this chapter).

Used only to illustrate how the flowchart can be applied, Table 7.1 takes the example of a generalised research project. Working step by step through

---

[3]For further details on 'Pathways to Impact' see www.rcuk.ac.uk/kei/impacts/ (accessed 9 October 2012).

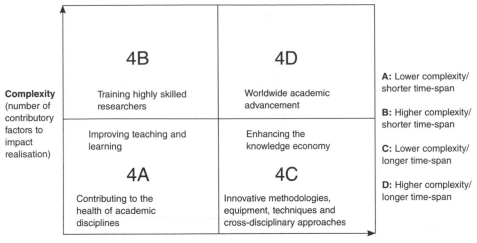

FIGURE 7.2 RCUK 'Pathways to Impact' academic impacts mapping

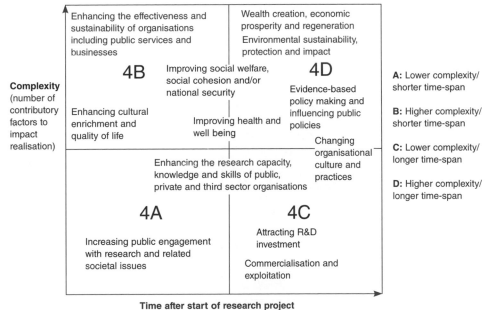

FIGURE 7.3 RCUK 'Pathways to Impact' economic and social impacts mapping

Figures 7.2 and 7.3 map the potential impacts of research highlighted by the UK Research Councils in their 'Pathways to Impact' against the time after a research project starts when a potential impact might be realised. Figure 7.2 shows academic impacts and Figure 7.3 economic and social impacts. This form of mapping can, for example, help understanding of the complexity of an impact to aid design of impact measurement, to illustrate complexity to stakeholders and qualify the level of attribution to a given activity realising an impact. For further details on 'Pathways to Impact' see www.rcuk.ac.uk/kei/impacts/ (accessed 9 October 2012). (Source: An adaption of Figure 5 in Bromley and Metcalfe, 2012)

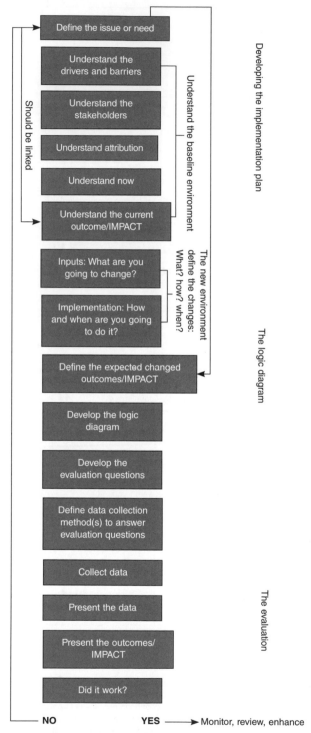

FIGURE 7.4 An evaluation flow chart encompassing the key elements of the methodology outlined in Chapter 7, expressed as a step-by-step process (see boxes 7.2 and 7.3 for key questions for an evaluator at each of the flow chart steps)

TABLE 7.1 Evaluation map – An evaluation map 'pro-forma' for evaluating the impact of a research project. Note this is a generalised construction used to illustrate how work-ing through the flowchart (Figure 7.4) leads to the development of an evaluation map for a project, in this case a research project with potential to influence public policy. The flowchart (Figure 7.4) asks the questions. The evaluation map records the answers. (Source: An adaption of Table 1 in Bromley and Metcalfe, 2012)

				Understand the baseline environment				Key implementation steps		Expected outcomes
	Issue	**Drivers for change — Carrots**	**Drivers for change — Sticks**	Barriers to change	Stakeholder needs/views	Attribution: Key influences	Now – key features/outcomes	Input(s)	How and when?	
Implementation plan (Logic diagram)	**The need to** e.g. why is the research needed? To develop greater understanding that influences public policy development in the area covered by the research project	**Carrots Why should I/we do this?** We need to know more to improve policy	**Sticks What happens if I/we don't?** Policy will be less effective	Several aspects of current policy	Current policy does not fully support need; expensive to administer	Wider economic/policy environment	Policy doesn't realise full potential	**Input(s)** *e.g.* Recruitment of researcher e.g. -grant application document -funding -experience/ knowledge -new investigations	**How and when?** *From receipt of funding*	**The research meets the identified need:** Understanding is developed and reflected in future public policy
Key logic steps to achieve outcomes (logic diagram for how research generates impact)				*0: Foundations* e.g. grant proposal; research expertise; team expertise; peer review of proposal. New investigations	*1: Reaction* Literature review; reflection/ hypothesis development; research planning; data/information collection	*2: Analysis/ Learning* Analysis of new information/data: increased understanding; new findings	*3: Dissemination* Papers/reports/ articles etc.; conferences; public engagement; public/ private sector engagement	*4: Outcomes* (From 'Pathways to Impact') *Understanding is developed and reflected in future public policy*		
Key evaluation questions/Logic step				Are the required expertise/knowledge/resources in place to start the research project?	Is the current environment understood? Has a new hypothesis been developed?	Has understanding increased? Has data analysis provided new information?	Papers published? Conference attended? Committees approached?	Is the new understanding reflected in policy?		
Evidence (tracking the development of impact)				0	1	2	3	4		
Example potential evidence sources/Key evaluation questions to 'answer' evaluation questions (✓ indicates evidence source could provide information) — Case study					✓			✓		
Focus group					✓	✓		✓		
Quantitative data				✓	✓		✓			
Other …				✓						

■ Shaded areas should link together in terms of content. Text in **bold** is common to any evaluation map.

the flowchart, an evaluation map for a research project can be developed, namely the flowchart (Figure 7.4) 'asks the questions' and the evaluation map 'records the answers'. Working through the flowchart step by step should support an evaluator in completing the evaluation map. A completed evaluation map should act as a good summary evaluation plan.

The understanding gained from using the described approach (Bromley, 2009; Bromley and Metcalfe, 2012) to evaluate impact has raised a number of key points regarding the methodology and its implementation that form a set of 'underpinning principles' (see Box 7.1).

BOX 7.1   GUIDING PRINCIPLES OF EVALUATING IMPACT

1. Know what the aim of any activity is at the outset. I.e. what is the identified need/issue/observation that led to the activity taking place? What impact is the activity designed to have?
2. Ascertain how the activity contributes to meeting the needs of different stakeholders, such as the needs of researchers, practitioners, the host organisation, the funders of the activity.
3. Build in evaluation from the start. Work through the logical thought process before designing any activity, so that evaluation is built in from the start and a logic diagram is constructed for how any new activity will logically lead to a desired impact. (The reality of how impact is realised may differ to some degree from the original logic but if there appears no logical connection between a proposed new activity and the realisation of the desired impact, achieving the impact is likely to be more difficult.)
4. Baseline assessment: know where you are starting from before you implement the activity to provide a means of comparison by which impact can be measured (e.g. do a baseline assessment, preferably at multiple impact levels). Understand the 'baseline environment' (see flowchart, Figure 7.4).
5. Respect the issue of attribution. Although direct causality is unlikely to be ultimately proven, consider what evidence can be collected to draw conclusions 'beyond reasonable doubt' and understand that this is a 'judgement' rather than an absolute.
6. Do not make a judgement based upon only one source of evidence. Acknowledge the potential for metrics to mislead when quoted as standalone figures. Collate both quantitative and qualitative information. Reinforce quantitative data with a narrative about the methodology that generated the data and supporting evidence of a qualitative nature.
7. Appreciate the potential subjective nature of the views of any people involved in any activity/process, etc. Always have additional supporting evidence when drawing conclusions from people's views.
8. Do not ignore the unexpected. Design and evaluate activity based upon the aims of the activity, but do not ignore unintended outcomes that become apparent during an evaluation. They may be valuable and help focus future or new activity.

The approach described does not consider evaluating impact just from the perspective of identifying 'additionality', which is a common practice. The approach identifies the current situation before any changes are made and then evaluates the impact the change made. The impact identified may or may not subsequently be viewed as additional since it may have qualitative elements – changes in nature rather than in number, size or frequency.

The approach also encourages evaluation to be built in to any activity before that activity begins. However, it is not uncommon for thought of evaluation to come after an activity has been implemented. The approach is still valuable in that it can still be used to analyse the current situation (environment) and define new or enhanced activity. It can also help in focusing future work. In any case, steps to guide the design and implementation of an evaluation, and the reflection upon its results, are discussed in the remainder of the chapter.

Object of study

This section discusses the basic actions involved in the selection of an object for study in an evaluation. Given the underpinning principles of Realistic Evaluation defined above, selecting an object for an evaluation study is reliant on the definition of the organisational strategy.

It is beyond the scope of this chapter to identify how particular organisations define their strategies. Nonetheless, good practice identifies that strategic orientation must be aligned with organisational vision statements (Turner, 2002). There are two possibilities here. On the one hand, the evaluating organisation may declare vision statements that have to do with the whole of its operations. As a consequence, the strategy for impact studies will have to be aligned with the broad goals of the organisation. On the other, it may also declare vision statements that are particular to its evaluation activities.

Specifically, the organisation must define the strategy that will guide one or a group of impact studies. There are three reasons for this.

First, the strategy offers the evaluator guidelines for the implementation of impact studies.

Second, it places the selection of the object of study in the wider strategic context of the relevant evaluating organisation.

Third, the strategy will guide not only the choice of an object for evaluation but also the aim of the evaluation.

Ideally the strategy for evaluation must be aligned to the vision statement of the organisation. The object is suggested here to result from a combination of the scale of analysis and the nature of the impact studied. For practical purposes, scale can be considered a consequence of the level of funding allocated to a given activity (Arnold, 2004). For instance, in an education activity, any impact evaluation deals with analyses that cut across different levels of funding scale. This can involve a single education activity on the one hand (e.g. evaluating funding for a specific teaching activity). At an intermediate level, it can also involve a group of teaching activities (e.g. evaluating funding for a number of related education activities, such as a module), or an education programme, a course for instance, combining a group of related teaching activities centred around a specific topic. On the other hand, it can involve funding to a specific education area that combines a number of teaching programmes (for example a department may support a number of courses related to a discipline area targeted by the organisation). It can also include evaluation of funding for the infrastructure that is required for the implementation of the education programmes (for example, laboratories and training centres) (Arnold, 2004).

In terms of the nature of impact, at each of these levels of aggregation, funding can have an impact of economic, social, cultural, policy or professional practice nature. The concept of variety in the nature of impact is evident, as articulated by Warry (2006) in terms of research funding. This approach is adopted in this chapter for application in more general evaluation activities. Therefore, whilst the object of analysis is influenced directly by the vision for impact evaluation of a particular organisation, it stems directly from the combination of the nature of the impact that will be evaluated and the scale of related funding for the activity.

The choice of an object for study is also related to the aim of the evaluation. There may be three main aims in undertaking evaluation: these are measuring impact, demonstrating impact or a combination of both (de Campos, 2010b; ESRC, 2009). Clarity in terms of any of these aims will result in clarity in terms of the type and phrasing of the question that the study will examine. In relation to demonstrating impact, evaluations may deal with processes, and hence relate to how impact develops, why it develops or what are the specificities of the impacts identified (Yin, 2009). For example, in an education activity, the evaluation may examine how a course influences the behaviour of students, or why behaviour is influenced or what aspects of behaviour are altered. In terms of measurement of impact, they may deal with questions about the intensity of impact (e.g. by how much a specific type of training altered, through changes in behaviour, a particular environment – say by saving a particular resource).

The object studied, the aim of the evaluation and the related questions should ideally allow the evaluators to have an idea about the results that are expected to emerge from the study. Once the object is defined, a review of the pertinent existing evidence should follow. This will reinforce a clearer understanding of expected results. Results will be even clearer in so far as evaluators have a degree of clarity about the variables that will be analysed in a logic diagram as discussed above, and the relationship between them and also about the methodologies that will be used to study the object.

In research methodology based on a positivist paradigm, expected research results are described in the hypothesis. Expected results should be aligned with the vision of the evaluating organisation. Unexpected results should also be designed into an evaluation strategy and contingency plans must be considered for these.

Once the vision and the strategy (encompassing the object of study, the aims of evaluation, and expected results) are clarified, the evaluator may consider how to validate them with stakeholders. This sort of feedback will enhance both the legitimacy and the robustness of the evaluation. In considering the underpinning principles of Realistic Evaluation, stakeholders may be involved in the evaluation from the outset. This means that the stakeholder can be involved at the point when an activity is designed. This aspect is developed further in the next section.

Key elements for a study

With reference to the underpinning Realistic Evaluation principle, the 'inputs' are the activities that effect changes to the environment and the logic diagram is ostensibly the mechanism that will realise the outcomes and impacts.

Figure 7.5 shows a logic diagram example for a learning process (Bromley and Metcalfe, 2008, but based on the ideas of Kirkpatrick and Kirkpatrick, 2006, and critiques of Kirkpatrick, e.g. Kearns, 2005). The diagram indicates: the input that changes the environment, that leads to a reaction from those engaged, which leads to learning, behavioural change and the final outcome or impact being realised. With this logic diagram, evaluation questions for each step emerge. For instance, what is the reaction of participants in the educational activity? Did they learn anything? Did their behaviour change subsequently? Were the original expected outcomes therefore realised?

The key elements for study centre on understanding the baseline environment. If the baseline environment is understood within the context of

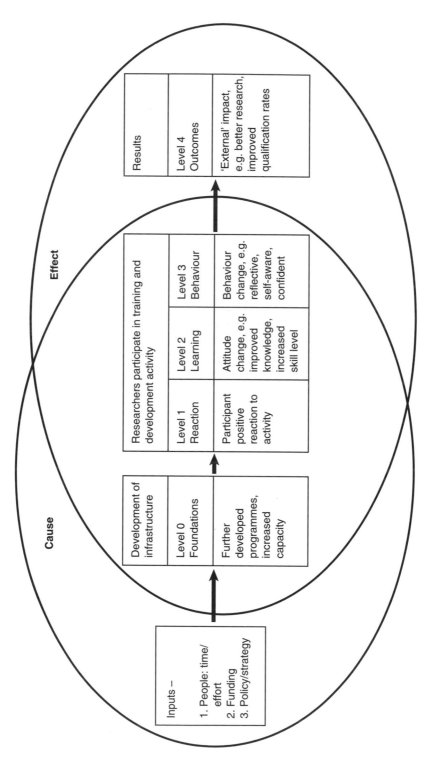

FIGURE 7.5 A schematic representation of a logic diagram for realisation of impact from an increased investment in training and development activity. This example relates to the UK investment in training and development for postgraduate researchers and early career research staff following the UK Government report of Roberts, 2002. (Source: Figure 1 in Bromley and Metcalfe, 2008)

the identified object of study then the new inputs can be designed with a view to the realisation of the outcome/impact.

Table 7.1 provides an 'evaluation map' that embodies the key elements of the approach outlined in this chapter (and aligns with the flowchart in Figure 7.4). An evaluation map can be constructed for any evaluation of impact by an evaluator and should act as a tool to foster a well thought out, logical approach to developing, implementing and reviewing activity that realises the expected outcome/impact.

With respect to each key element of the evaluation map (and/or Figure 7.4), an evaluator may wish to consider a range of questions as provided in Box 7.2 and Box 7.3.

BOX 7.2   KEY QUESTIONS FOR AN EVALUATOR WHEN DEVELOPING AN UNDERSTANDING OF THE 'BASELINE ENVIRONMENT'

The questions should be considered with reference to the flowchart in Figure 7.4.

Drivers or barriers for change

What are the current drivers? What are the drivers for change? Are there strong drivers? Are there barriers to change? Are there 'carrots' and 'sticks'? Within a particular area of work what is driving the area in the direction it is currently going? Will any activity designed to achieve an impact have to include an element that develops or enhances the drivers for change? Do any barriers need to be addressed?

Key stakeholders

Who are the key stakeholders? What do they want? Why should they support the change? What are their current attitudes and behaviours? Are their attitudes and behaviours supportive of achieving a desired impact? Will any activity designed to achieve an impact have to include an element that builds relationships or understanding with stakeholders?

Key external influences (attribution)

What are the key influences on the issue other than any activity you might do? What influences are in your control? Is there something so influential that it will challenge significantly the opportunity for success in achieving impact?

Understand now

What is the situation now for example in terms of structures, systems, number of people involved, investment level, technology, understanding, etc.? What are the current outcomes/impacts of what we do now?

BOX 7.3   KEY QUESTIONS FOR AN EVALUATOR WHEN DEVELOPING PLANS FOR A 'NEW ENVIRONMENT' FROM WHICH A NEW IMPACT WILL BE REALISED

The questions should be considered with reference to the flowchart in Figure 7.4.

Inputs

Having analysed the elements presented in Box 7.2/Figure 7.4, what changes are you going to make in respect of any issues identified from considerations of drivers/barriers, stakeholders' attitudes and behaviours, key influences, or anything else about what we have now, and so on?

   What are the new inputs (i.e. any activities, a new research project, training, etc.) to the environment that will logically lead to new impact?

Implementation

How and when are you going to make the identified changes?

Impact/outcomes

What do you expect the impact of your changes to be?

The study: implementation and reflection

This section discusses the implementation of the impact evaluation study. A starting point discussed in this chapter is to define a strategy and consequently an object for an evaluation. The evaluation strategy helps the implementation stage in two ways. First, it suggests a set of related actions and these should be further clarified during this stage. For instance, the nature of the activity considered in the evaluation strategy gives an idea of the nature of the impact that will be studied. Take the case of the UK Research Councils: research that is funded and evaluated by the Arts and Humanities Research Council is more aligned to the considerations of policy and professional practice impacts. Second, the evaluation strategy should give an *ex ante* idea of the type of evidence that will be needed, which in turn should help in the identification of the study question, the logic diagram and the methodology that will be used in the study. The latter aspect will be discussed in Chapter 8.

   As considered in this chapter, once the evaluation strategy and the object of study are clarified, the evaluator must decide on a suitable methodology that is relevant to the implementation of the study. In this section, we take the perspective of a study or a group of studies whose methodological selection will be undertaken at some point in the future. In any case, the evaluator must consider the management of the study from the perspective of its organisation in work packages, consider and manage risk issues and think about how results can be used for the purpose of reflection.

The first stage has to do with breaking the evaluation into more manageable tasks following standard project management techniques. A possible way to do so is to move from the more abstract to the more concrete elements. Therefore (being guided by the flowchart in Figure 7.4), one can start from the logic diagram based on the object of study, which then entails decisions about the method that will be used, which then points to the evidence that will be generated and ultimately to definition of a portfolio of studies (if that is the case). At the end of all of these stages, there could be reflection about what could and should be improved. Reflection can be intensified and formally carried out at the end of the strategy cycle.

This can be done following the work package approach exemplified in Box 7.4.

BOX 7.4   AN ILLUSTRATION OF A WORK PACKAGE APPROACH IN EVALUATING IMPACT

Work package label – definition of a logic diagram

The relevant tasks are: review of existing evidence to support the identification of key variables in the study; organisation of variables in the diagram, and determination of the cause and effect nexus between them.

Work package label – definition of evidence and methodology

The relevant tasks are: determine the type of evidence (e.g. qualitative or quantitative); and determine the study question and main methodology (see Chapter 8). If more than one study is considered, these tasks will point to a portfolio of studies. However, each study must also be designed in the context of its purpose (to demonstrate, to measure impact or both purposes) and the type of audience (e.g. policy-makers, end users or other stakeholders).

Work package label – definition of portfolio of studies

The relevant tasks are: working from the relevant study questions and attach suitable methodologies; use group of questions and related methodologies to generate an agenda of studies, and finally commission expert evaluators to assist in the implementation of

(Continued)

(Continued)

the studies. An optional stage in relation to this task is the implementation of a pilot study to test whether the evaluation strategy and the object of study are well articulated. This work package will generate the results of the evaluation studies.

Work package label – reflection

The relevant tasks are: prepare review document with results in light of objectives of evaluation; reflect on the match between results and objectives; use reflection in the preparation of next evaluation.

Once evaluation studies start to be completed, the evaluator will have a set of results. Two archetypal situations can be anticipated. On the one hand, these results can fit those envisaged when the evaluation strategy was conceived. On the other hand, the results can be unexpected and negatively different from those considered in the earlier stages. Of course, in either of these cases the evaluator must accept the results obtained. A pilot study is particularly useful to identify in the early stages of the implementation cycle which of these situations will prevail.

As a consequence of unexpected negative results, the evaluation strategy must incorporate the issue of risk. The evaluator, experts commissioned and stakeholders should be involved in risk assessment. Typical project management techniques here include the identification of the perceived risks, ranking them according to their capacity to disrupt evaluation strategies and acting on them, for instance conceiving contingency plans, to mitigate negative consequences (Turner, 2002).

With the results in hand, evaluators must set out to undertake reflection. The results can be consolidated in a document. The document may discuss whether the initial aims in undertaking impact evaluation were achieved, the extent of impact that has been demonstrated and what worked and did not work well in terms of the strategy. In particular, stakeholders and other parts of the evaluating organisation can be engaged in the reflection stage. The evidence gathered can be used to review the evaluation strategy implemented and to inform a review of the forthcoming rounds of evaluation strategy planning.

Conclusion

In this chapter we have attempted to provide guidance on a methodology for evaluating impact, setting out key concepts, themes and ideas. The methodology aims to foster a well thought out logical approach to evaluating impact which gives firm foundation to any evaluation. However, what has not been covered yet is how to actually apply the methodology in practice and gather evidence in an evaluation of impact. Chapter 8 overviews practical techniques for gathering evidence in an evaluation study.

References

Arnold, E. (2004) 'Evaluating research and innovation policy: a systems world needs systems evaluations', *Research Evaluation*, 13 (1): 3–17.

Bromley, T. (2009) *Evaluating Training and Development Programmes for Postgraduate and Newer Researchers*, London: Society for Research into Higher Education series Issues in Postgraduate Education: Management, Teaching and Supervision (SRHE).

Bromley, T. and Metcalfe, J. (2008) *The Rugby Team Impact Framework*, Cambridge: Careers Research and Advisory Centre (CRAC).

Bromley, T. and Metcalfe, J. (2012) *The Impact and Evaluation Group Impact Framework: Revisiting the Rugby Team Impact Framework 2012,* Cambridge: Careers Research and Advisory Centre (CRAC).

Buttrick, R. (2009) *The Project Workout: The Ultimate Handbook of Project and Programme Management*, 4th edition, London: Financial Times/Prentice Hall.

de Campos, A. (2010a) *Economic Impact Assessment Within the Research Councils: A Toolkit For the Evaluator*. Swindon: RCUK Strategy Unit.

de Campos, A. (2010b) 'A study on methodologies for research impact assessment: the response of the Research Councils in the UK to the Warry Report', *Industry and Higher Education*, 24 (5): 393–7.

ESRC (2009) *Taking Stock: A Summary of ESRC's Work to Evaluate the Impact of Research on Policy and Practice*. Swindon: ESRC. Available at: http://www.esrc.ac.uk/impacts-and-findings/impact-assessment/analysis-and-scoping.aspx (accessed 27 September 2012).

Kearns, P. (2005) *Training Evaluation and ROI: How to Develop Value-based Training*, London: Chartered Institute of Personnel and Development.

Kirkpatrick, D.L. and Kirkpatrick, J.D. (2006) *Evaluating Training Programmes,* 3rd edition, San Francisco CA: Berrett-Koehler Publishers Inc.

Pawson, R. and Tilley, N. (1997) *Realistic Evaluation*, London: Sage.

Roberts, Sir G. (2002) *SET for Success: Final Report of the Sir Gareth Roberts Review*, London: HM Treasury. Available at: http://webarchive.nationalarchives.gov.uk/+/http://www.hm-treasury.gov.uk/set_for_success.htm (accessed 9 July 2013).

Turner, S. (2002) *Tools for Success: A Manager's Guide*, London: McGraw-Hill.

Warry, P. (2006) *Increasing the Economic Impact of Research Councils: Advice to the Director General of Science and Innovation, DTI from the Research Council Economic Impact Group*, London: Department of Trade and Industry. Available at: http://bis.ecgroup.net/Publications/Science/ResearchCouncils.aspx (accessed 27 September 2012).

Yin, R.K. (2009) *Case Study Research: Design and Methods*, 4th edition, Thousand Oaks, CA: Sage.

8

HOW CAN IMPACT BE EVIDENCED: PRACTICAL METHODS?

TONY BROMLEY

In discussing methods this chapter will build upon the methodological ideas of Chapter 7 to consider four key points (with reference to the flowchart in Figure 7.4):

Key points

- Understanding the baseline environment which leads to identifying the need for and intentioned[1] outcomes/impact of any activity[2]
- Developing the evaluation questions
- Identifying appropriate data collection methods
- Presenting the findings of an impact study

Introduction

Clearly a comprehensive coverage of methods which encompass a vast range of ideas across subjects from social science, through arts and humanities to

---

[1]The unintended impacts of an activity should not be ignored and, as stated later in this chapter, the methods used to gather information in an impact study should be such that unintended outcomes can also be captured.

[2]Just to re-state the first footnote of Chapter 7, the word 'activity' is used here in a broad sense. To reflect your specific context 'activity' might be replaced by 'research project', 'project' or even 'intervention'.

the pure and applied sciences, is difficult within the confines a single chapter. This chapter, therefore, aims only to highlight some key methods within the broad headings of qualitative and quantitative data collection techniques relating to impact measurement, and introduces some key points to consider. For the novice researcher in qualitative/quantitative techniques of a general social science nature, this chapter should aid in the development of ideas on methods appropriate to gather evidence for a given impact study. Nevertheless, such a researcher is still encouraged to work, at least in the development stage of deciding upon the methods to be used to gather evidence in an impact study, with a researcher of expertise. For the experienced researcher in qualitative/quantitative techniques, this chapter should provide a 'framing' of the use of various methods in the particular context of impact measurement, from which the experienced researcher can consider the application of their knowledge of methods that may well have been applied in different contexts.

Understanding the baseline environment

As has been stated in Chapter 7, it is key in any impact study to have an understanding of the environment (or situation) before you implement any activity from which an impact is expected. Understanding the environment allows clear definition of the issue or need to be addressed and is the basis of following through the logic of designing and evaluating new activity that is focused on addressing the issue or need identified. A useful starting point is the desk-based review. For example, consider:

- What are the key points from published research for a given area?
- What are the latest related policy documents?
- What is the view from web-based discussion forums or special interest websites? What is in the general media domain?
- What are the experts in a given field saying?
- Who are the key stakeholders in your proposed impact study?
- What are the stakeholders particularly interested in?
- What are the key drivers in your area of study?

The review questions clearly depend upon the nature of the impact study but gathering information as widely as appropriate for a specific review is an important step.

For a major impact study it may be appropriate to consider more substantial review techniques but it must be recognised that this is not an insignificant undertaking. Two examples of more substantial reviews methods are systematic review (for a realistic approach to systematic review see Pawson (2006)) and meta-analysis. In systematic review the aim is to provide a comprehensive summary of available literature in a given area. Meta-analysis, for example, can synthesise results from numerous studies to identify themes or patterns.

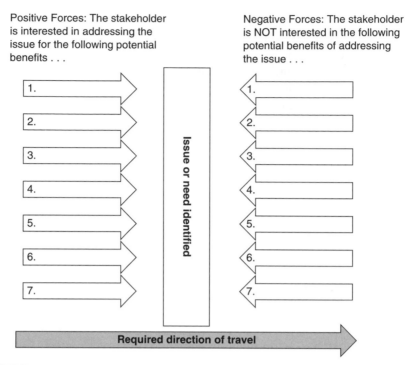

FIGURE 8.1 A force field analysis of stakeholders

It may also be appropriate to conduct interviews, focus groups and/or surveys (see below for details in respect of these methods) with stakeholders to gather further information.

As part of developing an understanding of the needs and drivers/barriers for stakeholders it can be useful to consider constructing a 'force field analysis' (after Lewin[3]) diagram to summarise key information drawn from a review in respect of stakeholder views. Figure 8.1 asks why a given stakeholder would be interested in your study and your target or intended impact, and also why they would not be interested. This analysis will support the design of an effective study.

Based on the review information gathered it should be possible and will be valuable to construct a 'mind-map' (Buzan, 2009) that shows the key influences in the area of your impact study. Figure 8.2 proposes, as an illustration, key influencing factors for the success of a researcher training and development programme.

Understanding the key influences allows a consideration of the attribution of any impact resulting from an impact study to the study itself rather than any external factor.

---

[3]Force field analysis techniques are credited to the psychologist Kurt Lewin.

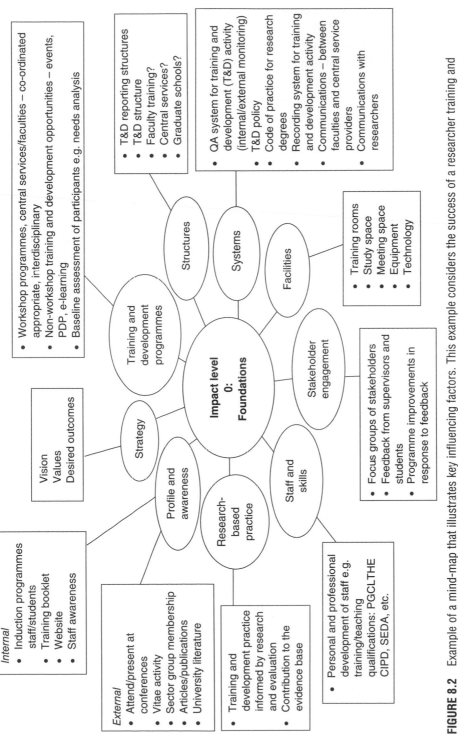

FIGURE 8.2 Example of a mind-map that illustrates key influencing factors. This example considers the success of a researcher training and development programme (Source: Bromley and Metcalfe, 2012)

When the review of the baseline environment is complete, the issue that needs to be addressed, along with the impact required, can be more clearly defined and focused. It may well be that some prioritisation is required as a review may highlight multiple issues with additional sub-issues. Prioritisation is best done on the basis of stakeholder needs. Who is/are the most important stakeholders and what are their priority interests? (And it may be you who is the most important stakeholder!) It is also easy to be over-optimistic and expect a new activity to have too wide-ranging and far-reaching impact(s) so any activity design and evaluation study should be done within a framework of realism based upon a good understanding of the baseline environment and an understanding of what is achievable with the resource available (human and financial) within a reasonable timeframe.

By the end of a baseline environment review there should be a good understanding of the environment now and the issues that need to be addressed (hence the impacts that need to be achieved). Consideration can then be given to new activity designed to achieve impact and the logic of how the new activity will achieve impact.

Developing the evaluation questions

Referring back to Table 7.1 and the evaluation map example (for a generalised research project targeting influence on policy), if we understand the issue/ need and the logic steps to achieve the outcome/impact we can consider the appropriate evaluation questions for each step of the logic diagram. Again this should flow easily and logically from the logic diagram. For example step 2 in Table 7.1 states logically that there will be analysis of new information which leads to increased learning. The evaluation question is therefore straightforward: 'Do we have increased learning?' We have the reference point of the baseline environment review against which to consider this question. Step 3 refers to dissemination. Again the evaluation questions is straightforward: 'Has there been private sector engagement?'

A common pitfall is targeting an impact that is not defined specifically well. For example, a target to enhance the 'employability' of a particular group needs further defining before designing an activity to achieve impact. This is because there can be multiple views of what 'employability' means.[4] The word needs to be 'unpacked' to provide something more specific.

---

[4]For example, Pool and Sewell provide a consideration of different definitions of employability and then suggest, 'Employability is having a set of skills, knowledge, understanding and personal attributes that make a person more likely to choose and secure occupations in which they can be satisfied and successful'. Lorraine Dacre Pool and Peter Sewell, (2007): 'The key to employability: developing a practical model of graduate employability', *Education and Training*, 49 (4): 277–89.

Again, for example, is it that people will be provided with development opportunities such that they have a wider range of defined skills which offers an opportunity for them to be employed in a wider range of roles or is it that more people will get jobs of any sort? In general, words such as 'employability' should be 'unpacked' into specifics before embarking on impact activity. The same would apply to exploring, for instance, the 'effectiveness' of an activity. Effectiveness can mean very different things to different people so it needs unpacking. Further, it may be the views of key stakeholders that are the best guide to such unpacking.

Identifying appropriate data collection methods

Box 8.1 provides a quick summary of the data collection methods discussed in more detail in this section.

BOX 8.1   A QUICK SUMMARY OF DATA COLLECTION METHODS AND CONSIDERATIONS OF THEIR USE

Qualitative techniques

Interviews: One to one. Structured or semi-structured? Need to be well managed. Keep on topic but allow interviewee to speak. Review and recap periodically to check understanding. Take care not to lead the interviewee with your questioning.

Focus group: Bring together a group of people. Needs good facilitation. Manage the dominant speakers to provide a platform for the less dominant speakers.

Observations: A researcher observes a set of events. Make clear your role to the observed. How involved are you? What difference might your presence make?

Quantitative

Surveys: Potential mass data collection method. Getting the questions right is key. Can be self-selecting. Usually needs significant effort to achieve good and representative response rates. May emphasise your interests over those of the respondent.

(Continued)

In a further example the Confederation of British Industry(CBI) website states, 'Employability covers a broad range of non–academic or softer skills and abilities which are of value in the workplace. It includes the ability to work in a team; a willingness to demonstrate initiative and original thought; self-discipline in starting and completing tasks to deadline'. Available at: http://www.cbi.org.uk/business-issues/education-and-skills/in-focus/employability/ (accessed 23 January 2013).

(Continued)

Indicators: Selecting and monitoring of a set of figures as indicators of impact. Can mislead if presented without a narrative. Can choose the wrong indicators that do not provide the information wanted. Attribution – figures might change due to factors outside the impact study.

In defining which data collection methods to use, it is important to consider addressing the issue of assigning attribution for an eventual impact to any given implemented activity. One approach to building in support for an argument of attribution when choosing data collection methods is to have elements of the data collection that follow through the logic diagram.

An example would be a cohort study. If an issue to be addressed is increasing the economic impact of research then a programme of activity could be designed including, for example, training and development of researchers in business development. Attendees at the training activity could be interviewed before they attend the activity for their views. After any activity they could be interviewed again or surveyed in respect of their views on their learning and finally they can be tracked in terms of any future business development. In terms of information to support assignment of attribution to an activity, you would in this case have initial views, views on learning achieved and then final outcomes of any business development from the group. In other words, a group of people has been monitored throughout the logic diagram. In general, in data collection for evaluating impact, include elements that track something (people in my example above) through your proposed logic diagram.

Another key consideration is that of scale. The scale of the data collection needs to be balanced with the available resource and the requirements of doing a robust impact study. For example, you may have multiple stakeholder groups who could have an interest in your impact study, leading to a potential group of, for illustration purposes, 1,000 people from whom you might want to collect data. If an individual interview is chosen as the data collection method, this is a substantial undertaking but has potential for an in-depth and rich data source to be gathered. Alternatively, an online survey could be used to gather views. The survey would be quicker and less labour intensive but the data gathered is unlikely to be as rich or in depth. Of course, one could also survey the 1,000 supported by a few 'sample' interviews, which would be a not unusual compromise. Even better might be a survey design that uses the language and issues revealed by a few in-depth interviews. Although the above examples are generalised, they do illustrate the need to take a data collection decision that balances the resource available against the depth of data collection required.

A third key consideration is whether you need qualitative information or quantitative information or both (i.e. a 'mixed methods' approach). A brief overview of qualitative and quantitative techniques is given in the following section.

Finally, it is very important to understand and respect ethical considerations in any impact study. Higher education institutions and research organisations will have ethics policies. It is good practice that no study is embarked upon or data collected until any ethical implications have been fully considered and the approach approved by the appropriate mechanism in an organisation. For example, when collating information from people, two very common concerns that need to be addressed are the ways in which information is recorded and stored and how it will be used. Again organisations should have policies on the appropriate method of storage of information.

Techniques producing qualitative data

By their very nature qualitative techniques can be subjective. In effect all techniques involve a researcher making some form of 'observation' to collect data and then making a judgement about or interpretation of those 'observations'. Factors such as self-selecting groups can come in to play, namely in considering whether the views of those who agreed to participate in interviews are representative of a population as a whole or are only representative of the population sub-group who will agree to do interviews. If a researcher could interview those who prefer not to do interviews they may well gain a different perspective.

It is important to consider at the outset qualifiers such as these and this may also lead to a decision that an impact study will gather information using qualitative and quantitative information (mixed methods) as each has limitations of its own. For example, quantitative information metrics quoted in a standalone way without an associated narrative can easily be misleading, as illustrated by the old saying about there being lies, damn lies and statistics.

Interviews may be structured or semi-structured or totally open and lacking in structure, the topic and structure being determined by the interviewee. The latter is not likely to be useful for evaluating impact since the researcher is seeking specific information on that topic. A structured interview is a very specific focused interview with a structured, defined list of questions allowing easier comparison between interviews; however, the approach can allow little room for the interviewee to raise issues important to them that may not have occurred to the interviewer. A semi-structured interview with a less defined structure or set of questions provides more freedom for the interviewee but can be more difficult to compare interview to interview.

Fundamentally the interview needs to be well managed. Basic points include:

- staying on topic politely but allowing an interviewee to speak;
- being careful not to lead an interviewee with the questioning style;
- taking opportunities to pause, review and recap at stages during the interview to check understanding and allow an interviewee to add any further points or clarification;
- at the end of the interview allowing time for an interviewee to add anything they feel has been missed;
- at the end of the interview to be clear to the interviewee about what happens next with the information you have gathered from the interview and over what timeframe.

Interviews take time. Transcribing and analysing interview information is also time consuming (a minimum of three hours transcribing for one hour of interview) although software systems are available to help. If you interview people at different times you may be able to build up a case study narrative for an individual that illustrates impact.

A *focus group* brings together a group of people at one time to discuss a particular topic or topics. The same issues as highlighted for interviews above hold for focus groups but the key obvious difference for the interviewer is the management of the group. For a group of around four or five people then a conversation in which all take part should be manageable. For larger group sizes the skill is more about facilitation, that is breaking a large group into smaller sub-groups, setting tasks for the monitoring of sub-groups, and then getting sub-group members to feedback to all. With a focus group, more views can be gathered in a shorter time span than for an interview but inevitably the information is likely to be of a lesser depth. The success of a focus group is likely to hinge on the skills and abilities of the facilitating interviewer to manage the group. Common management issues can be, for example, the presence of a dominant speaker (or speakers) whose views are brought to the forefront and, in a sense, the opposite of not giving space to the less dominant speaker so that their views can be heard. The skill of effectively managing a focus group should not be underestimated. When interpreting the data you need to consider the degree to which some participants might have conformed to the group viewpoint.

A researcher can conduct an *observation* of a set of events, record notes as events unfold and develop a view on what has happened. Researchers may be part of the event or stand away from it.[5] An analogy would be

---

[5]There is a philosophical point here. If a researcher is there, they are de facto part of the event whether they feel they are standing away from it or not.

that of the journalist. A common issue to consider is being clear to participants in an activity of the exact role of the researcher in recording information. Consider the kinds of questions that you might ask if you were a participant such as: 'Why am I here?', 'What is being recorded?', 'Why?' In addition as a researcher you need to consider how and in what ways your presence is influencing what is going on.

Reviewing documents is in a sense one step removed from the methods described above. Here a researcher will review available information not directly gathered by the researcher and form a view. There may be published records of interview transcripts, for example, or the minutes of meetings, or company reports. Review need not be restricted to text analysis. Analysis of images for example may also reveal valuable information. The qualifier is that, since the researcher is not the person who produced or gathered the information originally, it may not be clear how the information was produced or gathered, what oriented the focus of the production or gathering of information and what contextual issues influenced it.

Techniques producing quantitative data

Two areas are covered here, survey and indicators. Generalising, quantitative methods lead to the creation of numerical data and associated statistics. The key learning point is to always make available the narrative of how the numerical data or statistics were created. When a number is quoted in isolation it can easily be misleading. A simple illustration of this comes from the author's own experience of running a particular training and development activity. At the beginning of a three-day programme targeted at developing team-building skills, participants were asked to rate their skills and ability level on a ten-point scale for various aspects of team working. At the end of the three days, participants were again asked to rate their skills in the same way. The average number at the end of the three days was lower than at the beginning so that, in quoting the 'before and after' average numbers in isolation for the three-day programme, the impact of the activities seemed to be that participants' team working skills had got worse! From discussion with the participants, it appeared that what had actually happened was that during the three days participants became more aware of their own team-working skills and realised they had overestimated themselves at the beginning of the activity.

The *survey* offers the opportunity to gather information of a quantitative nature from a large group of people. It can also be used to gather qualitative information via the inclusion of 'free-text' options. Online surveys with automated data gathering capabilities can produce statistics very quickly from large groups. However, we do again have a few qualifiers. As for qualitative techniques described above, there may be a self-selection bias. We should consider whether we are surveying a representative group or the sub-group of people who will complete surveys. A further qualifier is in respect of response rate. If you send out surveys to 1,000 people and you get around 100 to 200 responses, this is not atypical. Therefore, there is a question about the validity of drawing detailed conclusions based upon responses from around 20 per cent of your target group. In a sense, these qualifiers are not major problems provided that they are understood and that any potential limiting effect is reflected in interpretations of, and judgements made about, impact. Also, as part of carrying out a survey, thought must be given to how the survey will be implemented and 'marketed' to maximise the response rate. (The effort required to generate a good response rate should not be underestimated.)

Much of the success in surveys lies in getting the questions right. All surveys should be piloted with small groups before being used on a larger scale. For example, when setting questions, it is not unusual to see unexpected answers because what might seem a perfectly clear question to a researcher may have some ambiguity to a responder. Both 'open' (no particular response suggested) and 'closed' questions (with a choice of responses presented) have potential to produce useful data in surveys but there needs to be some careful decision made about which sort of question and response is required for each section of the survey. Some basic points to consider are included in Box 8.2.

BOX 8.2   DESIGNING SURVEY QUESTIONS: POINTS TO CONSIDER

Open or closed questions: for example the following questions, all different versions of the same question, will be likely to gain different answers: Is it a good idea to host an Olympic Games?[6] (Yes/no answer options given.) What are your views on the benefits for a host nation in hosting an Olympic games? (A list of defined 'multiple choice' options given to choose from and responder asked to tick what they agree with.) What are your views on the benefits for a host nation in hosting an Olympic games? (Free text box provided for open response.)

 Repeating a question in a different form: in a survey there is potential for responders to respond in a way in which they feel they are expected to respond rather than necessarily

---

[6]Just to explain my choice of topic, as author I sit here in the UK writing this in the midst of the London 2012 Olympic Games and in the midst of debate about the legacy impact of hosting a games.

restricting themselves to just their opinion. Surveys can be designed to ask similar questions in a different way at different points in the survey to attempt to counter this possibility.

The **appropriateness of a yes/no** answer: this can provide a simple statistic that 'x' number of people 'agreed' or 'disagreed' with something, but tells little about extent of agreement.

The **appropriateness of a 'Likert-type'** scale: examples include providing the responder with the opportunity to express a view on a five point scale from 'agree entirely' with a particular statement through to 'entirely disagree'. You may want to consider providing an even number of choices because an odd number of choices does allow responders to select the usually neutral central option on the scale each time.

Beyond care in getting the questions right, further points to consider in surveying include those listed in Box 8.3:

BOX 8.3 FURTHER POINTS TO CONSIDER WHEN DESIGNING SURVEYS

Time effects: people need time to complete surveys. For example, attempting to survey a group from the financial sector as the end of the financial year approaches may well affect response rate. Also, if you implement an activity and survey a group immediately for their views on what they have experienced, you may get a higher response rate than if you wait for an extended period as recollections fade and people move onto other things. Conversely, the fewer responses received by waiting may be 'richer' as people have had time to reflect and perhaps implement some new ideas picked up from the activity you implemented.

Survey length: if the survey is too long it may deter people from completing it and also the responses from those who do respond may deteriorate in quality towards the end of the survey as attention begins to drift.

Survey fatigue: there are a lot of surveys out there. Your survey group may already have been surveyed many times by others and may be suffering from survey fatigue. This also relates to getting the timing of the survey right in terms of potentially busy periods in respondents' lives.

Comparability with other questionnaires or from another time: if you would like to compare your results to those from another questionnaire, say one conducted some time ago or before an intervention to note changes, you need to ensure that the same issues are addressed in the same language to give credibility to your deductions.

Gathering **qualitative information** in a survey: offering space for free text answers to questions allows qualitative information to be gathered via a survey. At the very least a survey should have a final free text opportunity for responders to add anything they want to say that they feel was not captured by the previous questions in the survey. Remember that you will need extra time and some expertise to code and interpret these responses.

Indicators

It is common to look to numerical indicators to develop a picture of, for example, performance. The particular aim of an impact study may in itself suggest a natural choice of numerical indicator or indicators that would define success. However, a key issue, apart from that previously described of the potential misleading nature of standalone numbers, is that of attribution. For example, an initiative to increase employability may be deemed to be a success and have had impact if the number of people employed in general across the economy goes up. However, without following through all that has been said in both Chapter 7 in respect of methodology and Chapter 8 in respect of method, the impact of a given activity is difficult to understand or attribute and any links might at best appear tenuous. That general employment has gone up might be a mere co-incidence and due to another factor or a combination of factors and might have no relationship to the initiative.

REFLECTION POINT

A speaker at a conference tries to persuade the audience that gross national product (GNP) rises with the number of doctoral students because countries with large numbers of them have a high GNP. What do you think? To what extent is this a logical, well-evidenced conclusion about the impact of doctoral students?

As well as the examples given above, examples of impact indicators might include numbers of participants in an activity. For instance, after the Olympic Games, are more people participating in a particular sport? In higher education, are more people graduating with on average a high class of degree? In medicine, has the success rate of a procedure improved? In business, have sales increased for a particular product? In each case, though, care must be taken about attributing causal links to correlation data, and to ascertaining other sources of influence.

Indicators are useful if they are considered with the other quantitative and qualitative information gathered for the impact study. If the impact of an initiative is not well understood, then the lessons for gaining further impact are limited.

Choice of method

In summary, in relation to the choice of method the decision usually centres on striking the right balance between the sorts of information you need to gather and the resource available to gather, analyse and interpret the information. The more information you gather about a potentially positive, attributable view of the impact of your activity, the more confident you can be about claiming its value. However, this does take time, so a question is, 'How confident do you need to be in your impact claim?' or potentially more importantly, 'How confident do your stakeholders need you to be?' Your selected methods of gathering evidence referenced against the evaluation questions developed from the logic diagram will constitute an evidence gathering strategy for your impact study. (This is the bottom section of the evaluation map in Table 7.1.) Box 8.4 provides some summary tips in designing your data collection approach.

BOX 8.4 A FEW QUICK TIPS FOR DESIGNING YOUR DATA COLLECTION APPROACH

- The intended impact needs to be well defined. Unpack words like 'employability' or 'effectiveness' with stakeholders.
- Make sure the approach establishes an understanding of the baseline.
- Track something as it progresses through the logic diagram to support claims of attribution.
- Keep a good balance between depth of study and needs of stakeholders (inevitably you cannot do everything!).
- Collect qualitative and quantitative information.
- Make sure you respect ethical considerations.
- Understand the 'qualifiers' for your chosen data collection methods.
- Consider how you will present your findings.

Presenting findings

How to present the findings of an impact study is a crucial consideration. Working through the methodology described in Chapter 7 alongside the methods approach highlighted in this chapter should provide a comprehensive narrative to support the findings of your impact study as a thorough evaluation. Ultimately, however, the final conclusions of an impact study will be a judgement based on evidence gathered. When findings are presented to a stakeholder it is usual for a stakeholder to want to know that the study had rigour but they seldom wish to see absolutely every fine detail of the theoretical background of the methodology and methods used to collate information. As a researcher or impact evaluator you need to be able to provide the appropriate level of information needed by a given stakeholder.

In summary, following the methodology described here provides a number of components that can be presented within a 'package' as summarised in Box 8.5.

BOX 8.5   THE 'PACKAGE' OF INFORMATION THAT COULD BE PRESENTED TO STAKEHOLDERS IF THE IMPACT EVALUATION APPROACH DESCRIBED IN CHAPTERS 7 AND 8 IS FOLLOWED

A completed **evaluation map** (Table 7.1) providing summary detail for each key component of the impact evaluation methodology with reference to your impact study.

Key **points of evidence** against each evaluation question which is referenced against your logic diagram (lower section of Table 7.1) for the study.

A review of the baseline environment.

A **force field analysis** of stakeholder interests (Figure 8.1).

Your evidence gathering strategy mapped against evaluation questions which are drawn from your **logic diagram**.

A **mind-map** (Figure 8.2) that illustrates the potential influences on your impact study and illustrates how you can attribute impact to your study.

The framework of **guiding principles** for the impact methodology listed in Chapter 7 (Box 7.1).

References

Bromley, T. and Metcalfe, J. (2012) *The Impact Framework 2012: Revisiting the Rugby Team Impact Framework*, Cambridge: Careers Research and Advisory Centre.

Buzan, T. (2009) *The Mind Map Book*, London: Pearson Publications.

Pawson, R. (2006) *Evidence-based Policy: A Realistic Perspective*, London: Sage Publications.

9

WHAT SKILLS ARE NEEDED TO BE AN IMPACTFUL RESEARCHER?

JENNIFER CHUBB

Key points

This interactive chapter discusses:

- The types of skills, attributes and dispositions a researcher may possess
- Communicating research to different audiences
- The Pathways to Impact document – what skills are required to increase your impact potential?
- Your skills in relation to a training needs analysis
- The support and guidance available to support skills development in relation to impact – university infrastructures and national agencies

Introduction

There is an increased demand from the funders of research, and those measuring outcomes for the purposes of assessment, for researchers to be able to identify and articulate particular impacts of both their proposed research and past projects. Researchers are therefore required to move out of their traditional comfort zone to consider much more how they might engage, sell, promote and inspire others outside the academic environment with their research. For some researchers, the skills needed to be 'impactful' are perceived as being new and the desired attributes are not always those associated with the traditional perception of 'the academic'. However, the culture within universities is changing and researchers are increasingly becoming more comfortable with the idea that the skills for effective knowledge exchange and impact can be harnessed and developed with the support of their peers and through institutional infrastructures (see Chapter 10). This chapter will illustrate that, whether you wish to stay in academia or not, the skills for developing impact will help you whatever your chosen career path. Indeed by harnessing your existing skills and exploring ways in which you can maximise your potential through researcher development and teamwork, you can start to move towards becoming an 'impactful researcher'.

Transferable skills

If you were asked the question 'What skills and attributes do you traditionally associate with the role of a researcher?' responses might include:

- Researchers are experts in a particular area.
- They have good project management skills.
- Researchers are good at coming up with new ideas.

… among other potential responses.

The assumption that the skills one might normally associate with researchers are somewhat at odds with the skills associated with impact could be seen as a myth.

Let us take for example the three responses I mentioned earlier.

Expert in a particular area – if a researcher is someone who is seen as an expert in a particular area then it stands to reason that the expertise and its associated knowledge may well be of benefit to others whether inside or outside the academic environment. For example, researchers are called upon to act as expert witnesses, consultants and advisors to a range of different audiences outside the university environment because of their credibility, so being an expert on a topic has potential for considerable impact.

Project management – many researchers develop strong project management experience through being awarded grants and carrying out associated tasks such as managing finance and teams. It is therefore possible that these skills could be useful when managing other types of projects outside academia, such as perhaps those relating to the commercial world. The skills involved in project management are transferable and might well be used when working with end users of research.

Good at coming up with new ideas – since researchers are focused on developing new ideas and are skilled in working in ways which contribute to new areas of knowledge by pushing boundaries, so too it might also translate that such abilities could lead to new innovations, and/or changes in products and services outside academia.

These examples highlight that it is important to consider more broadly how the skills you already possess can be developed and nurtured in order to maximise your potential for impact. However, for many researchers there will still be areas that require attention in order to maximise the chance for real success in relation to impact.

Whilst researchers can and should be harnessing their existing skills, organisations set up to support the career development of researchers are also keen to ensure that the community has special skills that equip them to respond to the requirements of the Impact Agenda. As well as understanding the role of transferable skills, attention has been given to introducing the concepts of engagement, influence and impact into researcher development from the outset of the doctoral training experience and beyond. This chapter will discuss the skills necessary to engage with a range of audiences and will also consider the Pathways to Impact document, which is included in grant applications.

What skills do I need?

It is important to remember that impact can be understood in different contexts. Impact could be categorised as:

Forward looking/future impact (grant applications)
Current impact (dissemination activities to wider audiences)
Past impact (assessment and marketing)

Future and current impact – grant applications and dissemination

The need to consider the answers to three key questions relating to impact in grant applications requires researchers to make a real effort to consider ways in which they can engage with external audiences.

These three questions are:
Who will benefit from the research?
How will they benefit?
What will you do in order to allow them the opportunity to benefit?

It is important to be realistic when addressing these questions. Depending on who you are hoping to engage with and what the purpose is for that engagement, there could be a variety of different ways in which you might approach them so that they might benefit.

ACTIVITY 9.1

Have you considered what skills and attributes you will need to develop/harness in order to make a success of your potential partnerships with beneficiaries? Jot down some ideas about the types of skills you envisage as being important in order to make an impact.

It is important to consider your own skills development when embarking on your impact journey – researchers asked to respond to a question about skills required for impactful research gave some of the answers outlined in the lists in Box 9.1. This data is taken from a qualitative research project which explored attitudes and barriers to impact.

The following responses outline just a handful of skills and attributes perceived to be of importance by researchers. You might consider how far these correlate with your perceptions.

BOX 9.1   SKILLS AND ATTRIBUTES REQUIRED FOR RESEARCH IMPACT

Attributes	Skills
Drive	Social skills
Motivation	Networking
Clear intentions	Communication
Vision and enthusiasm	Quantitative and qualitative research skills
Ability to build trust	Developing a 'sales persona'
Entrepreneurism	Teaching and presentation
Performing outside comfort zone	Self-promotion
Being competitive	Persuasion and influence

When asked to reflect upon issues around skills for impact, researchers from the same study also made the following comments (the broad subject background of the individual respondent is given for each quotation):

'It's a hard job with teaching and administration to then be asked also to suddenly develop an extra persona where you are selling yourself.' (Science)

'I get a huge buzz out of trying to communicate to a wider audience, winning arguments and seeing them used – it's not their use that motivates me, it's the process – I'm a competitive soul!' (Social Science)

These responses show a range of perspectives demonstrated by researchers in relation to skills for carrying out impact activities such as working with the public, policy-makers or business and industry. The first response could be seen to reinforce concerns that the traditional skill set of the academic is somehow at odds with the skills required for impact, whereas the latter response reflects much more of a sense that researchers feel increasingly at ease with the Impact Agenda (though they may have different ways of engaging with it). Everyone will view their own skills and capabilities differently. However, understanding where your strengths and weaknesses lie can help you focus on the areas you need to develop to improve your chances of successful collaboration and innovation.

It is not just the challenge of identifying potential impact that requires us to evaluate our skills. This may also be the case for researchers considering the impact of past projects where our existing skills can once again be utilised in order to support our impact story.

Past impact – assessment and marketing

The need to consider the impact of previously carried out research is of growing importance. This is reflected in the Research Excellence Framework assessment exercise where there is a significant weighting on 'impact' (20 per cent) required in submissions. Here, researchers are asked to develop structured narratives backed by meaningful indicators about the research project, what its impact was, how far it reached non-academic audiences, how significant it was and, importantly, how this can be evidenced.

Though the skills we have already discussed broadly apply to impact within this context, it could also be argued that the most important categories of skills and abilities for responding to this requirement include the following:

- research skills – looking for evidence of impact;
- communicating with past and current partners;
- story telling – writing up a convincing narrative;
- evaluating the effectiveness of partnerships.

Though not exhaustive, this list of skill categories highlights that some of these areas overlap with the skills we traditionally associate with researchers.

In support of the specific and transferable skills of researchers, the national organisation Vitae has developed a framework, designed in consultation with a range of stakeholders, which highlights the types of skills and attributes researchers might possess in order to make a success of their chosen careers. This is called the Researcher Development Framework (RDF).

The framework is depicted in the RDF wheel, consisting of four domains all dedicated to a particular skills area of which impact and engagement is one. An illustration of the RDF can be found in Appendix II.

You will see there that Domain D specifically focuses on the types of skills and attributes required to work with others to ensure the wider impact of research. It relates to all types of impact previously outlined in this chapter (Vitae, 2012), although impact is not the only aspect of research in which these particular skills are important.

The Researcher Development Framework states that in order to maximise opportunities for impact, researchers should be able to work with others, communicate, disseminate and engage different audiences. In doing so, they will be better placed to work in teams, influence others, collaborate and/or carry out public engagement, enterprise, and policy activities.

ACTIVITY 9.2

Thinking about the Researcher Development Framework and the views expressed earlier in this chapter, consider your skills in relation to your impact goals. Think carefully about what you want to achieve.

How will you maximise opportunities to achieve research impact? (Activities to bring about impact might include public engagement activities, setting up a business and/or starting a dialogue with policy-makers.) Consider the skills you feel you need to develop and jot down some ideas about how you might go about making steps towards achieving your goals.

You might find it helpful to draw up two columns: the first headed 'Impact goals', the second headed 'Skills to develop'.

Having looked at the skills perceived by researchers to be important for research impact (both in terms of retrospective, potential and current impact), we will now take a closer look at how these skills and attributes come into play within particular circumstances.

Pathways to Impact

Impact can be achieved by exploring a number of different pathways. A diagram produced by RCUK illustrates the different pathways or routes to achieving impact – see Appendix III.

For the purposes of this chapter, let us take a look at three broad areas which encompass many of the ideas listed in the diagram.

Commercialisation – setting up new products and services

Public engagement – engaging, inspiring and consulting the public with research

Policy influence – taking research outcomes to policy-makers and contributing to debate

Whilst the specific skills needed in order to reach out to different audiences will depend upon your purpose for engagement, drawing out the skills and potential attributes required in different scenarios can help you to consider areas you might need to develop.

Scenario one

John is a postdoctoral researcher in the department of computing at a research-intensive university. John has developed a computational technique that can process an image that contains pictures of people's faces in order to detect the number of people in the picture as well as several parameters for each of the people it detects, such as their age, gender, ethnic group, facial expression (smiling, frowning, etc.) and the presence or absence of a beard or glasses.

John has yet to develop a business plan for his idea, but this will broadly outline:

- the product, its unique selling point and the expertise of his team;
- the market he wishes to enter, including information about competitors showing robust analysis of the market;
- the intellectual property (IP) issues surrounding the opportunity;
- financial matters relating to the product – how much investment is needed and for what return – in other words, what is in it for potential investors?

ACTIVITY 9.3

Consider and list the skills John will need to harness in order to write this plan and make a successful pitch to the investors.

Scenario two

Sarah is working in the department of social work on teenage pregnancy and perceptions of young mothers and their rights. Having carried out preliminary research, Sarah is now looking for funding to develop a public engagement forum in order to consult and involve public views in her research. Sarah wants the forum to run every three months over a twelve-month period and will need to advertise this to potential delegates. Sarah is also hoping to form an advisory group made up of young mothers, members of the public and policy-makers to help to further inform the piece of research with a view to influencing policy debate around this issue.

In order to carry this forward, Sarah will need to:

- gain public interest in her project;
- contact policy-makers;
- make arrangements for hosting the events;
- prepare briefings for the advisory group.

ACTIVITY 9.4

As above, consider and list the skills Sarah will need to harness in order to develop her ideas and make these connections.

Although both scenarios involve working with different audiences and for different purposes, an exploration of the broad skills necessary to maximise the potential for impact are contained in Box 9.2 (note this list is not exhaustive).

BOX 9.2   THE BROAD SKILLS REQUIRED TO MAXIMISE THE POTENTIAL FOR IMPACT

Team work	Self-promotion	Self-belief
Persuasion	Negotiation	Project management
Research skills	Empathy	Sales
Communication	Influence	Presentation
Leadership	Confidence	Organisation
Enterprise	Ability to summarise complex messages	Planning
Cultural awareness	The ability to think outside the box	Enthusiasm

---

So, how does this relate to developing pathways to impact?

Addressing the Pathways to Impact document and impact summary

Research Councils UK require the inclusion of impact summaries and Pathways to Impact documents in all grant applications. Once you have reflected on the skills of carrying out impact activities, it is important to assess the appropriateness of the activities you wish to undertake. Having done so, you are then required to articulate this in a written document so that you might convince the funders of research that this is a project that is *value for money*, both in terms of its *academic excellence* and its *relevance to society and the economy*.

The Pathways to Impact document and summary, like an REF impact narrative case study or a policy document, must be a skilfully constructed, concise, jargon free and engaging document. It should be clear and specific, backed by a strong track record or evidence of your chances of success – here, your purpose is to win funding, so those reading about the impact of your research need to feel convinced of the following:

- the appropriateness and relevance of the beneficiaries and routes to engagement proposed;
- the chances of success in carrying out the suggested activities to maximise impact;
- the benefits identified in the summary to wider society.

Reviewers of Research Council grants will assess the impact of the project based upon two documents. (Please note, most funders require some detail regarding dissemination, outputs and public engagement but the specifics of this can vary. The following relates specifically to RCUK funding councils – you should refer to your funder guidelines when preparing your proposal to find out how they are addressing this section.)

Impact summary – this is a statement which forms part of the J-eS form about the potential impact of the research to be funded. It includes details of the kinds of beneficiaries outside the academic community and outlines the ways in which they will benefit. As a guide, this should not exceed 4,000 characters and should be written in jargon-free language as though communicating to a non-academic intelligent audience (RCUK, 2011).

Pathways to Impact – this two-page document addresses the activities you will undertake in order to maximise your project's opportunities for impact. The Pathways to Impact document gives details of relevant and appropriate activities, which may include non-academic conferences, commercial strategies and/or public engagement events. It will be important to show how these activities might be evaluated and to provide an idea of when you will carry these out over the course of the project (RCUK, 2011).

Putting your skills into action

When addressing the question of impact it is important to reflect on the following:

- Who *might conceivably* be interested in your research? (We communicate with different audiences for different reasons.) What are you trying to achieve?
- What characterises each group of end users? What are their specific requirements and needs?
- What is the purpose of your engagement? What do you want to achieve?

Let us assume that you have identified certain end users who might be interested in your research and believe there are real potential impacts, which could arise from building relationships with these beneficiaries. It is important therefore to consider the perspective of your potential partners or collaborators. For example, your potential audience will vary in relation to their level of education, their age, their degree of interest, their level of prior knowledge and their reasons for caring in the first place.

Defining your message

You will need to define your message for different audiences. Consider:

- What do you want people to know?
- What do they need to know to understand that?
- What do you wish to get out of the engagement?

Tailoring your message

You then need to establish what you want to say and how you wish to work with these beneficiaries. The following are considerations to make before communicating to different audiences.

Use clear accessible language.
Use appropriate terminology (no jargon!).
Try to demystify your work.
Take your time over your message.
Believe in your message.
Sometimes, you need to 'sell' your research.

Promoting yourself and your research

Having identified the potential beneficiaries of your research project, it is vital that you turn your focus to thinking about what the end user wants and needs. Whether your identified beneficiaries are found in industry, the policy world or are members of the public, they will be interested in knowing what is in it for them or perhaps, rather, how it might affect them. Therefore, you must present your work in terms of the *'benefits'* to end users as opposed to talking about the *'features'* and the academic detail. For the purposes of this discussion:

A 'benefit' can be defined in terms of what the product or service does specifically for that particular end user or customer.

A 'feature' refers to the describing information of a particular product or service.

It is important to remember that people buy benefits, not features. You need to 'sell' the benefits rather than talking about the features of a product or service. Knowing the difference and harnessing this skill will stand you in good stead for creating strong and meaningful partnerships for mutual benefit.

What are the potential challenges?

There are various challenges associated with communicating your research to different audiences; you need to therefore be mindful of the potential issues or challenges present, summarised in Box 9.3.

BOX 9.3   SOME POTENTIAL CHALLENGES WHEN COMMUNICATING WITH DIFFERENT AUDIENCES

Characteristic differences between researchers and business/industry:
- Industry/policymakers/publics may not have scientific backgrounds.
- Researchers tend to use language which is very complex or esoteric.
- External organisations have different expectations.
- The business and policy-making world work to different time scales from academia.
- Researchers have to build credibility with end users – this can take time.
- Researchers may feel they lack the confidence and skills necessary in order to engage with end users effectively.

Anticipating risk and recognising the potential barriers associated with communicating to different audiences can help you plan for impact more effectively.

ACTIVITY 9.5

Consider your own research. Who might feasibly be interested in your research outside the academic environment and how will it make a difference to them? Spend some time

(Continued)

(Continued)

considering the activities that might be appropriate in order to bring about the desired impacts. You might find it helpful to list your ideas under the following questions.

Who will benefit from the research? How will they benefit?

What will you do to ensure they have the opportunity to benefit?

Writing about your plans for impact in this way can present many challenges. It is a skill in itself – keep practising by jotting down ideas as they arise. It can also help to show a friend or a colleague your plans and ask for feedback in order to gain new perspectives on your work.

Finally, a key skill of impact must surely be the ability to summarise research for a lay audience.

ACTIVITY 9.6

In no more than 100 words, what would your lay summary be?

Training needs analysis and support for skills development

This chapter has examined how important the role of skills development is within the context of this agenda. You can find a wealth of information about training needs analysis and the development of transferable skills in another volume in this series: *Developing Transferable Skills*, Denicolo and Reeves (2013), but we will provide here some basic information to guide your further explorations. Whilst researchers may naturally possess certain skills and attributes, moving into new environments and working with diverse organisations can present its own challenges.

It is very important therefore that you consider the importance of your own skills development during your research career. One way to encourage this is to carry out your own training needs analysis (TNA) (sometimes alternatively labelled either learning needs analysis (LNA) or development needs analysis (DNA)).

Training needs analysis (TNA)

The aims of a TNA are to:

(a) identify the relevant skills and knowledge you have developed in your academic career to date and show how you have developed them.
(b) identify the skills/knowledge you will need to develop and/or acquire in order to become a more impactful researcher.
(c) identify what training is required in order to develop additional skills/knowledge.

ACTIVITY 9.7

Let us look at your own training needs. Where do you feel your strengths lie in relation to this agenda? Spending some time reflecting on the skills and attributes you possess and the areas you need to work on will help you as you develop your ideas for research impact. Remember, as described in Chapter 6, skills for impact might also be bought in through working with consultants and specialists as appropriate. These can be built into the costs of a grant if you have considered where that expertise needs to come from. You could use the following headings to guide your reflection and begin an audit and action plan:

- Relevant skills and knowledge you have developed and how you have developed them.
- Skills/knowledge you will need to develop and/or acquire in order to become a more impactful researcher.
- Identify what training is required in order to develop/acquire the additional skills/ knowledge.

How can I get support with my skills development and build confidence in this area?

It is important to remember that impact often arises through team work, collegiality, collaboration and communication with numerous partners, so by understanding your own skills and capabilities you can figure out what role you can play in contributing towards achieving impact. In taking things forward, most universities provide support through staff and researcher development provided centrally. However, bespoke and departmental/school focused training is often also available. Universities also have support functions that can help you with specific issues relating to your skills development. These may include:

Research/enterprise and innovation offices: these offices support the commercial potential of small and larger-scale research projects. They are staffed traditionally with support staff in business development roles whose expertise comes from having held positions in industry and commerce.

Careers service: these offices serve to support the broader career development of students and staff at universities. Whether or not you wish to pursue a career in academia, the careers service will be able to help you to consider the ways in which you can harness your skills to improve your employability.

Alumni services: skills development can take many forms; hearing from your peers about their career choices and experiences can help you to make informed decisions about the choices you make.

Further information

For support with your skills development outside the university, the following agencies can support you:

Vitae: this is a national organisation supporting the career development of researchers: www. vitae.ac.uk

National Coordinating Centre for Public Engagement: the centre promotes good practice and sharing of ideas about how universities can engage with the public for mutual benefit: www.publicengagement.ac.uk/

The Association of Graduate Careers Advisory Services (AGCAS): http://www.agcas.org.uk/

UK Council for Graduate Education (UKCGE): www.ukcge.ac.uk/

Research Councils UK (RCUK): most Research Councils' websites have information on developing pathways to impact and related considerations. These include impact toolkits and support information.

For more information on training for those looking to develop skills in the areas relating to research innovation and impact, visit the Knowledge Transfer Portal of the RCUK: http://www.rcuk.ac.uk/kei/ktportal/Pages/home.aspx

For more information on transferable skills and how to develop them to your advantage, you could consult another book in this series: *Success in Research: Developing Transferable Skills*.

References

Chubb, J.A. (2011) 'The impact agenda and academics' perception of their roles: perspectives from the UK and Australia'. Manuscript in preparation: unpublished thesis.

Denicolo, P. and Reeves, J.D. (2013) *Success in Research: Developing Transferable Skills*, London: Sage.

RCUK (2011) 'RCUK impact requirements frequently asked questions'. Available at: http://rcuk.ac.uk/documents/impacts/RCUKImpactFAQ.pdf

RCUK (2012) 'What do the Research Councils mean by impact?' Available at: http://www. rcuk.ac.uk/kei/impacts/Pages/meanbyimpact.aspx

Vitae (2012) 'Researcher development framework'. Available at: www.vitae.ac.uk/rdf

10

HOW CAN KNOWLEDGE EXCHANGE SUPPORT THE DEVELOPMENT OF IMPACT THROUGH PARTNERSHIPS AND UNIVERSITY INFRASTRUCTURES?

ANDY JACKSON

Key points

- The concept of knowledge exchange as a potential route to impact
- Clarifying and articulating the purpose of your research impact
- Understanding the journey from research to impact
- 'Selling' the benefits of your research to non-academic audiences
- Identifying, understanding, prioritising and engaging external partners and stakeholders
- Support services for knowledge exchange and impact in university research

What is knowledge exchange?

Through the 1990s, the process of linkage between the academic researcher and those outside the university sector was widely seen as a one-way transfer of expertise, whereby insights gained through the university research community would be 'handed over' to those in the 'real world' to be put to good use in products and services. Since the publication of the Lambert Review of University–Business Interaction (HM Treasury, 2003), this view has evolved to reflect a much greater depth and breadth of engagement that we see reflected in the research Impact Agenda today. More recently, the 'Review of Business–University Collaboration' (Wilson, 2012) made further recommendations about the development of organisational support structures and led to the Council for Industry and Higher Education announcing, in June 2012, plans to launch a National Centre for Universities and Business. The report emphasises the value of networking between university staff and their counterparts in industry, and highlights the importance of facilitating these links. The concept of knowledge exchange embodies this vision and encompasses both the systems and processes by which a two-way flow of people or ideas is achieved between the research environment and non-academic organisations, for mutual benefit.

Why is knowledge exchange important?

In a fast-moving world, organisations must adapt and evolve to respond rapidly to the changing needs of their customers, funders or beneficiaries. Organisations cannot rely on the notion that a single technology or service capability is enough to ensure a sustainable and successful future.

As a consequence, the key asset of any business or institution has become the knowledge at its disposal and its ability to deploy this knowledge to address new challenges. These capabilities and resources may be held within an in-house staff base, but managers are increasingly looking outside their own organisational boundary for new sources of knowledge, technology and information.

The term 'open innovation' (Chesbrough, 2003), promoted in a book of the same name, is based around the notion that however successful your organisation may be, 'not all of the smart people work for you'. If organisations collaborate by combining their knowledge, technology and experience in the development of new products and services, the results can be much more sophisticated than any single organisation could achieve (at least without a massive investment). These networks of collaborators may include representatives from industry, academia, government or third sector organisations with mutually reinforcing capabilities. This trend for organisations to reach out to external sources of expertise means that, in recent years, universities have played an expanding role in supporting public and private sector organisations in the development of new products and services.

These trends drive a need for greater integration both across internal (for instance, between university departments or faculties) and external boundaries (linking with external organisations). Policy-makers and research funding bodies have responded to this through the introduction of cross-disciplinary funding schemes, a focus on collaborative research and the concentration of funding into smaller numbers of larger projects (allowing major cross-organisational, multidisciplinary projects to be supported from a single source).

The result of this is that university managers and policy-makers are increasingly taking account of the views of their external collaborators to inform both their research and teaching priorities, and there is now a greater emphasis on the need for forming relationships with external partners, often across multiple points of contact within the university setting. Case study 10.1 shows how a multifaceted collaboration can develop over many years between a university and an external collaborating organisation.

CASE STUDY 10.1   IBM AND THE UNIVERSITY OF YORK

For over a decade IBM have developed a broad strategic relationship with the University of York, initially based around research collaborations in computer science, but branching out to link with a wide range of touch points in the institution from the Careers Centre (IBM are a major employer of graduates from across the university's departments) to departments as diverse as Environment, Psychology, Philosophy and Electronics. As a result of this collaboration, IBM and the University of York have developed a number of joint research projects ranging from small, early-stage investigations to multi-million pound programmes spanning many years. Staff members from IBM sit on industrial advisory panels at the university, directly contributing to decisions around curriculum and research management and fostering a two-way exchange of ideas between the business and academic environment. In 2011, a team of IBM researchers relocated to the Department of Computer Science on the University of York's recently opened campus extension. The relationship is supported by a structured memorandum of understanding, setting out mutual goals and, crucially, defining points of contact in each organisation to allow rapid formation of new links to address specific opportunities in a responsive way.

The growth of interdisciplinary research

The successful development of new products and services can involve interactions with science and technology as well as people, organisations, governments and numerous other stakeholders. In this environment, projects are increasingly positioned at the interface between pure, applied and social sciences. Furthermore, the desire to tackle issues and develop ideas in new, innovative ways draws in thinking and inspiration from the arts and humanities. The case studies presented here (10.2, 10.3 and 10.4) give examples of how interaction between academic subject areas and across organisational boundaries can provide innovative solutions and insights to address real-world research challenges from technology to public policy.

CASE STUDY 10.2   IMPROVING THE IMPACT OF THE HOME ELECTRICITY MONITOR

The development and widespread availability of low-cost home electricity-usage monitors in the late 1990s was viewed by some as a promising development in the drive to reduce unnecessary energy usage. Since this time, systematic studies have indicated that although such devices have an initial impact on consumer behaviour there is a downtrend in attention to the monitor over the first few months of use, leading to a diminished long-term effect. Solving this issue has been the subject of subsequent research and development work, examining the effect of more technologically advanced devices that combine real-time information on energy usage with web-based reporting and other innovative forms of feedback. The end goal of a low-cost solution that is effective in the long term can only be achieved through a cross-faculty effort, combining software and hardware engineering skills with a detailed understanding of human behaviour gained from expertise in psychology and sociology.

CASE STUDY 10.3   'OPEN ARCHIVE: THE MINERS' STRIKE: A CASE STUDY IN REGIONAL CONTENT' (AHRC, 2007)

This collaborative research project was funded through the AHRC/BBC Knowledge Exchange Programme's pilot funding call, also known as KEP. The aim of the Arts and Humanities Research Council/BBC KEP was to develop a long-term strategic partnership bringing together the arts and humanities research community with BBC staff to enable co-funded knowledge exchange and collaborative research and development. This project investigated how the BBC uses its archive holdings via the Open Archive. It examined how the BBC deals with its regional audiences and how regional rather than national news and historical agendas might be prioritised to provide these audiences with material that can be used to explore memories of significant events in their own lives. The project also examined how archivists and broadcasters deal with ethical issues raised by sensitive or contentious material and explored ways in which these materials need to be contextualised for future use. The study was based on the major historical event of the Miners' Strike (1984–5) and focused specifically on how various categories of material, including news, documentary and dramatic reconstruction represented this strike, and how they might be used within communities directly affected by it and its long term consequences. The outcome of the study led to policy advice for the BBC. The benefits from the outcomes and outputs of these projects should be of equal significance to both partners.

> ## CASE STUDY 10.4   'PHILOSOPHY INFORMING PUBLIC POLICY AND DEBATE' (AHRC, 2012)
>
> The extraordinary developments of the biological sciences over the past 50 years have had a major effect on our wider understanding of science, while raising complex questions around identity, responsibility and human dignity. Genetics, for example, has become an increasingly important area of philosophical research. Professor John Dupré from the University of Exeter led a project that investigated these developments, and also trained young researchers in the philosophy of biology.
>
> Impacts included:
>
> Informing public policy, including through giving oral evidence to the House of Lords Science and Technology Committee Inquiry into Genomic Medicine.
>
> Helping to develop public understanding of the biological sciences.

Is knowledge exchange synonymous with research impact?

In the academic community there is a perception that those funders involved in encouraging and supporting impact have a tendency to narrow their focus onto commercialisation and economic impact. The concept of knowledge exchange provides a broader context in which to frame the processes by which research outputs find their way into products, services and policy, and offers a helpful mindset in which to consider how economic, societal and cultural impact can be achieved. It does not, however, encompass all possible routes to impact and it is important to consider the entire context of how funders and policy-makers define impact, and use this to inform how you approach the issue in your own research practice.

What is the purpose of your research impact?

The policy environment around research impact is geared towards encouraging academic practitioners to develop a conscious approach to ensuring their research has the maximum possible 'real world' influence by embedding impact from the outset of the research design process. As explained in Chapter 6, this ethos is built into the process by which grants are awarded, projects are managed and overall research excellence judged. Consequently, it is important that as a practising researcher you approach the question systematically, to consider what impact your research may ultimately have and to understand and consciously plan the processes by which this will be achieved.

In what follows, we consider two models for research impact. The first is focused on the development of a new product or service that builds on the outputs of research; the second examines the process by which research findings influence policy.

How do ideas develop from the research environment into products and services?

It is important to note that the terms *product* and *service* should be interpreted very broadly and that the processes described here can be applied equally to the development of a textbook, a museum exhibit or a new aircraft engine (albeit with varying degrees of complexity, risk and cost). The diagram in Figure 10.1 illustrates the process taken by many businesses and universities in taking ideas and applying them to the creation and improvement of services and products.

Any developmental project has some inherent risk: a new technology may not turn out to work as well as expected when deployed in a real-world setting. A public performance may not attract the audience you hoped for and external factors such as a lack of funding or the actions of competitor could adversely affect your success. The graph in Figure 10.1

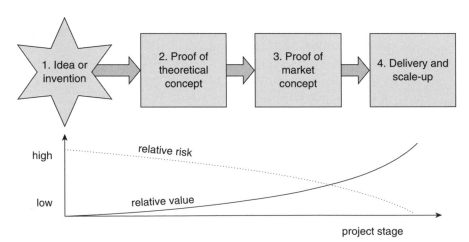

FIGURE 10.1 Developing a new product or service from the outputs of research

shows how a properly designed development project will gradually elimi-
nate these risks and, over time, drive up the value of the project.

The stages of development are shown in Box 10.1:

BOX 10.1   THE STAGES OF PROJECT DEVELOPMENT

1. The process starts with an idea or invention. This may be a discovery in the lab,
   or the birth of an idea for a musical performance or literary publication. This often
   has inherent value (especially if you have reason to believe that your idea could
   lead to socio-economic impact and that you are the first person to think of it), but
   also substantial risk, since you are unlikely to have demonstrable proof of its
   viability.
2. At this stage, you should focus on establishing whether the theoretical concept has
   the properties you originally envisaged. In the case of a piece of technology, this
   normally involves building a laboratory demonstrator that shows the new idea
   working in practice. If the idea relates to the development of a theatrical or musical
   performance, you may decide to spend time at this stage assessing whether it is
   feasible to gain access to performers with the necessary skill, the required equip-
   ment and an appropriate venue and whether these would allow the idea to be
   realised in practice.
3. Once confidence has been gained that your idea is fundamentally sound, you must
   establish whether there is a genuine demand for the end product or service. It is
   important to think not in terms of features of your new development (for instance,
   a light source that consumes 50 per cent less energy than the best currently
   available) but to frame its value in terms of the potential benefits to the key
   stakeholders – often an end customer or consumer (following the example above,
   flat panel TVs that consume almost half the energy of those on the market
   today – both reducing electricity bills for the consumer and benefitting the
   environment for society).
4. Your project should now be at a stage where sufficient confidence has been gained to
   develop and deliver a new product or service. Often, and particularly if investors are
   involved in the project, strong emphasis is given to the achievement of scale –
   whether through mass marketing of a product or the expansion of a service nationally
   and internationally.

Why is it important to consider risk?

Each stage of a project carries some risks.

Risk and value are important because they help us to view the project
from the perspective of an outsider, whether that is a partner or investor in

the project, an attendee at your event or an end-user or customer. Many of these stakeholders will be interested in seeing that you have properly understood the risks involved in the development of your idea, and that you (or your partners) have a viable plan for addressing them.

Note that the horizontal axis of the risk/value curve in Figure 10.1 is not time, but project stage. This is because it is not necessarily the case that the project will progress in a linear fashion over time and it may at times fall back a stage, for example if an idea proves unworkable in practice, or a competitor appears in a market that makes your idea obsolete before it is launched. It is the maturity of the idea and the proximity of its realisation that gives it value, not how long you or your team have been working on it.

Beyond ideas, products and services, how can research contribute to policy?

Research can make an impact when it is used to shape public policy. Unrestricted to subject area, though often associated with the natural and social sciences, researchers from a diverse range of areas may find that there are public policy implications arising from their work which they wish to explore. This can take many forms: acting as an expert witness, shaping legislation through providing evidence, contributing to the understanding of policy issues and reframing debates are just some of the potential impacts arising from communicating with the policy-making environment. RCUK defines impact as the 'demonstrable contribution that excellent research makes to the society and the economy by 'increasing the effectiveness of public services and policy' (RCUK, 2012). The Research Councils are keen to encourage researchers to interface with the policy-making environment and see this as a viable route to achieving impact. In response, many researchers have started to consider ways in which to engage with the policy-making environment, by considering what kind of communications strategies they might use and which processes they might adopt in order to achieve the best results.

There are, however, many challenges ahead of you when you set out to influence policy. The policy-making process is complex and generally iterative; it can therefore present potential obstacles when we try to ascertain exactly what piece of evidence has played a part in the process and when. However, appreciating this will help you construct a fluid approach to your goal of influencing policy.

Some other challenges often cited by those trying to influence in this way include concerns over the fact that the policy-makers themselves rarely come from an academic or scientific perspective – as described in Chapter 9, you will need the skills of being very clear and precise in explaining complex ideas to those in a position of power to do anything meaningful with it. Thus working on presenting your work in the most accessible way is crucial to increasing the chances of having your ideas taken seriously. The potential for conflicting, often hidden agendas within the policy arena (see Chapter 5) might also act as a barrier for your ideas being taken up – building strong relationships and being mindful of these issues will therefore stand you in good stead when working in this way.

Where do I start?

If you are starting from scratch, consider how you present your work – policy-makers are essentially a non-specialist intellectual audience – communicate in jargon free, accessible language and keep interactions brief and to the point whether you are writing a short document or conversing over the phone. Relationships are built over time, and so perhaps you might start at a local level – building rapport with civil servants in the policy field informally or formally to help you find routes to the right people.

For advice on these routes, a document issued by the Natural Environment Research Council (NERC) 'Science into Policy' (NERC, 2013), can be used as a very helpful source of support. This report represents the policy-making process as a cycle (shown in Figure 10.2) in which policy decisions evolve through successive iterations involving the monitoring of their impact and the environment in which they have influence. As a researcher, you may have the opportunity to contribute at many stages throughout this cycle, whether through the development of evidence resulting from primary research, or the provision of expert advice in the processes that underpin options and risk analysis or the effective implementation of new policy decisions.

External partners and partnership working

Working in partnership with external organisations can make a huge difference to the speed and success of your research impact ambitions. External partners can provide funding, experience, complementary technology and knowledge to help with the development of your ideas. Although not exhaustive, the diagram in Figure 10.3 categorises the range of external partners that typically engage with the university environment.

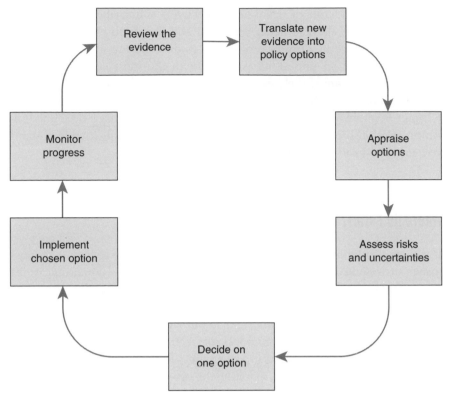

FIGURE 10.2 The cyclic process of policy development and review, adapted from 'Science into Policy', NERC, 2011

External partners will tend to focus their interest on specific stages in the development of an idea (although often they will be interested at more than one stage); depending on their specialism and the type of interaction you are aiming for, the following are potential partners or collaborators.

1. Investors and funders are often crucial to the success of a project. Throughout the process set out in Figure 10.1, it is common for each step to require funding. This may come from sources internal to your institutions (for example, challenge funds, pump-priming or proof-of-concept grants), or externally (such as venture capitalists, angel investors or grant funding bodies). These organisations will be interested in the success of your project, often because their own success depends on it. Investors expect a return on their investment and, as well as the size of the return, will also be interested in how long it will be before they are able to realise their investment (usually by selling shares in a spin-out company, or receiving profit-related revenues when a project comes to fruition). Although they would rarely expect a financial stake in the results of research, some public-sector funding bodies

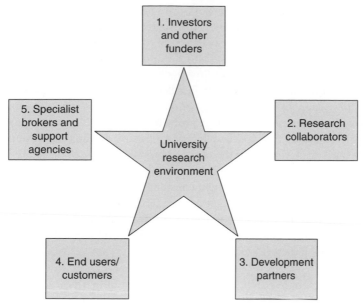

FIGURE 10.3   Classification of partner organisations in the university environment

require reporting on the impact of the work they support – often against clear quantitative measures (see Chapter 8) such as the creation of jobs or the generation of income.

2. Research collaborators fall into several sub-categories. As explained earlier in this chapter, the research environment is becoming increasingly interdisciplinary and competitive by nature. This means that researchers are increasingly called upon to collaborate with colleagues in other academic departments in their own institution, with those in another university, or with researchers in the businesses community, charities or social enterprises.

3. The development of a new product or service is a specialist task and often demands capabilities that are not commonly found in a university (such as designing a product to be ergonomic, robust, reliable and easily tested, or liaising with manufacturing plants in the Far East). In cases where such expertise is helpful, universities often collaborate with specialist partners that have this expertise.

4. Ultimately, the achievement of research impact always depends upon successful engagement of an end-user, whether that is a customer buying a product (in turn driving economic impact), or a member of the public attending an educational exhibition or lecture. Gaining a proper understanding of the motivations and interests of these stakeholders, and tailoring the development of your ideas to meet these is critical if you are to successfully maximise the impact of your research.

5. The university environment contains many specialist organisations dedicated to supporting knowledge exchange. These organisations help with the

formation of partnership networks, the joining of researchers with funders and investors, the identification of experts who can plug skill gaps in your team or the provision of expert advice to help you to develop your ideas. They may be publicly funded and thus provide their services free of charge or at a subsidised rate. In relation to the creation of new products/services arising from the use of university intellectual property (IP), organisations such as IP Group (www.ipgroupplc.com) and Fusion IP (www.fusionip.co.uk) have been set up to generate a profit by taking a stake in the success of a project (usually through the allocation of shares or the sharing of profits or revenues from the sale of the eventual product or service) in return for their support. Some organisations in this category offer publications (often available online at no charge) giving the researcher useful insight into the processes of innovation and knowledge exchange. For example, Cartezia (http://www.cartezia.com/) in conjunction with the Technology Strategy Board (TSB) have published a paper exploring some of the challenges of early stage business development (Phadke, 2010).

In many cases, single partners may fall into several of the categories above. For example, a commercial research partner may also be interested in putting some investment into the project in return for a share of future profits, and may also be in a strong position to help with productisation of a technology to make it suitable for manufacture and sale on a large scale.

ACTIVITY 10.1   IDENTIFYING POTENTIAL PARTNERS

Consider which external partners you might involve in your own research work. You may wish to start this exercise by looking at the types of organisations that colleagues in your faculty or department already engage with.

How do I identify and engage external partners?

Once you have established the types of external partner that would be useful to support your research impact objectives, the next step is to identify the relevant points of contact within these organisations and form links to them. Often, you will be able to get help with this process from staff within your institution's research support team.

It is often also possible to identify new potential partners through your own online research and by making direct contact yourself, even if that means making a cold call to their switchboard. To maximise your chance of success, ensure that you can express clearly and succinctly what is really unique about your idea, technology or proposal. The key to success here is to prepare carefully and be resilient and persistent – accepting that you may need to make several approaches before finding the right partners. Every interaction generates new knowledge and understanding, so do not be disheartened if you receive a negative response from some organisations or individuals.

What makes a successful partnership?

Partnerships work best when:

- All partners achieve mutual benefit from the relationship.
- There is clarity in how communication links operate between partners. It can be useful to identify individuals in each organisation who will act as single points of contact with responsibility for directing enquiries between the partners.
- There is clarity around what each partner is aiming to achieve through the relationship. Many organisations find it helpful to capture this understanding in a memorandum of understanding: a non-binding agreement that has no legal standing but provides a single point of reference and a means to articulate the objectives of the collaborating parties.
- There is trust between the partners. This is earned over time by the behaviour of the representatives from the respective organisations, but it is also important to remember that most reputable organisations will operate ethically by default (for example, by honouring the terms of contracts and being honest when calculating royalty payments).

What are the benefits of knowledge exchange?

ACTIVITY 10.2   BENEFITS OF PARTNERSHIPS

Based on your own research area and work, list the benefits of partnership working from the perspective of the university and from the standpoint of the external partner.

- Benefits for the university
- Benefits for the external

Support services in the university sector

Successfully navigating through the processes described in this chapter requires the combination of academic and research capability with complementary business and commercial skills such as:

- Business planning
- Financial analysis and modelling
- Investor engagement
- Contract development and negotiation

These support the researcher's efforts to engage with external partners and work collaboratively to achieve impact from their work.

Internal sources

In the last decade, most universities (at least in the UK) have developed specialist support units to assist with this amalgamation of expertise. In many cases, these began life with a relatively narrow brief of supporting technology licensing and the formation of spin-out companies aimed at taking forward the commercial development of an idea.

In some cases, these 'knowledge transfer' offices were founded as (or transitioned to become) completely separate trading arms, either wholly owned by the host university, or with investors taking a stake in the business in return for funding.

An example of this model is ISIS Innovation Ltd, a wholly owned subsidiary, established to lead on the commercialisation of intellectual property and development of consultancy projects from the research base of the University of Oxford and, increasingly, to offer its expertise on a commercial basis to other researchers in both the public and private sector worldwide.

Many universities also maintain an in-house capability for the development of commercial activity and engagement with external partners. In recent years, recognising the benefits of aligning support for pure research and knowledge exchange activities, a number of institutions have formed Research and Enterprise offices. In some cases this has been strategically driven by the research Impact Agenda. There is also recognition within institutions of the increased emphasis placed by funders and policy-makers on supporting collaborative research, and the concentration of research funding increasing the importance of very large projects that inevitably require central co-ordination and support.

External sources

Beyond your institution, several initiatives and funding schemes exist specifically to support knowledge exchange. You will normally be able to get advice from your in-house team on which of these is appropriate for your work and how to access funding. One of the most successful and long-running programmes is the Knowledge Transfer Partnerships (KTP) scheme, administered by the Technology Strategy Board. This provides matched funding to cover the cost of a research associate working on a specific project to forge links between an academic research group and an external organisation. The scheme is developmental by nature and provides funding to support the personal professional development of the associate and cover the time of an academic supervisor. For more information on KTPs visit www.ktponline.org.uk.

ACTIVITY 10.3   YOUR KNOWLEDGE EXCHANGE PLAN

Consider how you could begin to develop a knowledge exchange plan for your own area of research by addressing the questions below:

- What are the key products, services or policy domains into which your research could have an influence?
- Based on the earlier exercise, who are the key partners (or types of partner) you would like to engage with over the next 12 months?
- What are the key messages you would like these partners to know about your research work?
- What approaches will you adopt to engage with them?
- Who will you approach (both within your institution, and externally) to support your knowledge exchange work?

Useful web links

You may find the links below helpful as you explore the range of bodies that support knowledge exchange in the UK and work with those involved in building links between universities and outside organisations:

- Technology Strategy Board (for information on the KTP programme and other knowledge exchange initiatives) – www.innovateuk.org

- UK Science Park Association (bringing together science parks and innovation centres) – www.ukspa.org.uk
- Cross-council Research Programmes (RCUK's thematic research challenges) – www.rcuk.ac.uk/kei/ktportal/Pages/xrcProgrammes.aspx
- The UK Intellectual Property Office – www.ipo.gov.uk
- The National Endowment for Science, Technology and the Arts – www.nesta.org.uk
- The Association for University Research and Industry Links – www.auril.org.uk
- The RCUK knowledge transfer portal – www.rcuk.ac.uk/kei/ktportal/Pages/home.aspx
- The Department for Business, Innovation and Skills – www.bis.gov.uk
- The JISC Business and Community Engagement programme – www.jisc.ac.uk/whatwedo/themes/bce.aspx
- The National Coordinating Centre for Public Engagement – www.nccpe.ac.uk

References

AHRC (2007) 'AHRC/BBC knowledge exchange programme summary of awards 2007'. Available at: http://www.ahrc.ac.uk/Funding-Opportunities/Documents/ahrcbbcsummaryawards.pdf

AHRC (2012) 'Examples of economic impact from AHRC-funded projects', Arts and Humanities Research Council. Available at: http://www.ahrc.ac.uk/Funding-Opportunities/Documents/Examples of Impact from projects.pdf

Chesbrough, H.W. (2003) *Open Innovation: The New Imperative for Creating and Profiting from Technology*, Boston: Harvard Business School Press.

HM Treasury (2003) *Lambert Review of Business-University Collaboration*, final report. Available at: www.lambertreview.org.uk

NERC (2013) 'Science into policy'. Available at http://www.nerc.ac.uk/publications/corporate/policy.asp

Phadke, U. (2010) 'Building innovative businesses: the triple chasm model'. Available at: https://connect.innovateuk.org/c/document_library/get_file?p_l_id=6501519&folderId=6518335&name=DLFE-64821.pdf

RCUK (2012) 'Knowledge exchange and impact'. Available at http://www.rcuk.ac.uk/kei/Pages/home.aspx

Wilson T. (2012) 'A review of business–university collaboration', Crown, Department for Business, Innovation and Skills. Available at http://www.bis.gov.uk/assets/biscore/further-education-skills/docs/w/12-610-wilson-review-business-university-collaboration

11

HOW CAN YOU BECOME
AN IMPACTFUL RESEARCHER?

ELLEN PEARCE AND PAM DENICOLO

This chapter summarises key themes from the earlier chapters through the journey of what impact means, why it matters, how can you create and measure it, when is it evident and what skills you need and what resources you can draw on to be competent at it. It also aims to address the individual dimension and explore a range of potential ways for you to consider your own role and relationship with the Impact Agenda.

Impact, in its simplest definition, is about making a difference. More specifically, impact in the research context is the influence, effect, demonstrable contribution, change or benefit that results from the research. This can relate to the economy, public policy or services, cultural capital and society generally.

REFLECTION POINT

Chapter 2 addresses some of the wide-ranging motivations individuals have for undertaking research. The real questions to consider are 'What does impact mean to you in relation to your research?' and 'If your research could make a difference, what would that difference be?'

While the current Impact Agenda is driven by the funders of research, it is the individual responses of researchers which will determine what happens on the ground to research outcomes, and this, arguably, is what really counts.

It is the changing nature of, and emphasis on, research through the recent introduction of the notion of 'impact' as a relevant and scoreable part of gaining research funding which has led to concern within the academic community. In Chapter 1, it was argued that the Impact Agenda sought to make explicit what had previously been implicit; research by its very nature has led to breakthroughs in all areas of study and life for centuries. However the debate has been most strongly fought over issues such as academic freedom and whether the increasing focus on outcomes and impact will erode the value and funding for curiosity-driven research which, by its very nature, is not undertaken in the context of a practical route to impact.

At the 'core' of the impact issue are individuals: researchers and academics who navigate their way through an ever-changing funding landscape. In the rhetoric and media coverage that surrounds the debate it is easy to forget the very unique motivations and perspectives of, and responses to, this emerging agenda from a diverse group of academics. You will need to find your own perspective on the issues outlined in this book and be able to defend and debate your views. There is an argument, articulated in Chapter 4, that suggests that given its importance, it is essential that, as a researcher, you are able to understand and articulate the impact (or not!) of your research to a wide range of stakeholders.

Perhaps, in our view, the most important impact or outcome of the research process is the development of highly trained individuals like you, capable of bringing the impact of your research training to a range of employment settings, careers and society more widely. The Research Councils explicitly value this as an output of their significant investment in research and early career researchers, recognising that over 60 per cent of the doctoral researchers they fund each year will move from higher education, taking their skills into the wider economy (http://www.rcuk.ac.uk/kei/Pages/SkilledPeople.aspx).

In a Vitae study 'What do Researchers do? Destinations and Impact Three Years on' (http://www.vitae.ac.uk/wdrd) doctoral researchers were surveyed three years after they received their doctorate. Not only does the research outline a unique employment pattern for those with a research background, but it also indicates that doctoral researchers are able to have a unique impact in the workplace through engaging in research activity, using their skills and knowledge and being innovative. It also explores how their doctoral training has an impact on their wider lives through developing fulfilling careers, enhancing social engagement and improving the quality of life. Three years after graduation, 19 per cent were working in research roles in higher education and 22 per cent in teaching in higher education.

So we return to the question of how to become an impactful researcher. The Vitae Researcher Development Framework (RDF) was developed from first principles, by researchers for researchers, and it articulates the knowledge, behaviours and attributes of successful researchers. The RDF is for planning, promoting and supporting the personal, professional and career development of researchers in higher education. It was developed through interviews with successful researchers at various career stages, from doctoral researcher through to professor, and was validated through an expert panel of senior academics working across a spread of disciplines, institution types and geographical locations (www.vitae.ac.uk/rdfmethodology).

The Vitae Researcher Development Framework has four main domains, one of which is 'Engagement, influence and impact'. This is further broken down into three sub-domains, covering 'working with others', 'communication and dissemination' and 'engagement and impact'. These in themselves are complex areas, and it is likely that you will want to prioritise some aspects within this domain as particularly pertinent or useful to you in

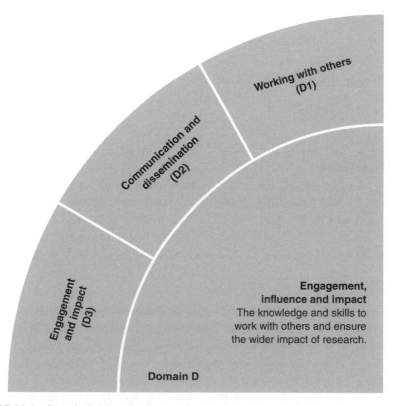

FIGURE 11.1   Domain D, Vitae Researcher Development Framework

achieving your own vision of an 'impactful researcher', depending on your current level of experience.

REFLECTION POINT 〜〜

Consider the areas of Domain D of the Researcher Development Framework in Appendix II and highlight those that resonate with you. They could be areas where you have a track record of experience or expertise, or they could be areas where you would like to gain experience or expertise. Consider what it would take to develop these skills further or put to into action.

It is clear from the definitions of impact discussed in Chapter 1, and the requirements of the various research funders outlined in Chapter 6, that there are a wide range of outcomes that have credence as research impacts. There is therefore scope within disciplinary contexts, as described in Chapter 4, and within the context of the research area for a range of potential impacts which can also play to personal strengths and motivations. Research impact can range from major changes in government policy to setting up a local community group, from filing patents to setting up a social enterprise. Clearly you need to engage with colleagues within your research group if appropriate but, as there are so many potential aspects to research impact, choose those which you can be genuinely passionate about and committed to.

REFLECTION POINT 〜〜

Consider the areas of the Researcher Development Framework in Appendix II that resonate with you. If they are areas where you would like further capability or experience consider creating an action plan to do so. This is not something that others can do for you, so becoming an impactful researcher is down to you and your motivation to fulfil this (see Chapters 3 and 9).

Winning funding is a key part of being an independent researcher. Therefore, you could chose to become an expert in speculation about the impact of your work. Think widely and openly about possibilities. Most research funders will publish the criteria they use for assessing impact on their websites so you can think deeply about whether you could meet them and how. Consider the costs associated with assessing and demonstrating impact as mentioned in Chapter 6. Funders will want to see that you have a realistic implementation plan to build your understanding of impact and that you understand the purpose of the impact assessment. Chapter 5 highlights that much of the predicted impact can happen many years after the initial research so it is important to gather baseline data and to anticipate where impact might be in order to set up the right measures as discussed in Chapter 7.

Given the current emphasis on being able to demonstrate the impact of research in order to secure funding, most universities and research centres will have support available (see Chapter 9) to early career researchers to help you build your competence and confidence in navigating and responding to these themes. Building relationships with internal and external partners and collaborators will also help you on your way (see Chapter 10). Have a look at what is on offer and consider building your capacity to engage with the Impact Agenda as part of your career development plan, particularly if you want to pursue a career in academia.

It seems to us that much of the potential success of researchers in responding to the Impact Agenda is about being open to possibilities and curious about the future directions not just of your research but also the potential applications of your research. Just as many argue there is a seren-dipitous nature to research, and to careers, we argue it follows that this is also the case for research impact.

CASE STUDY 11.1 BUILDING ON RESPONSES

Dr Helen E. Lees, TheoryLab, School of Education, University of Stirling

My research has been working with the idea of silence and its applications in schooling. Many teachers find there is a lack of silence practices and awareness and wish to use this valuable educational resource to improve behaviour and attainment but also help their students attain and maintain peaceful calm for well-being. It was this need of others to know more that led me to set up a website to accompany my recent monograph on the topic – mainly for people who want quick access to the ideas and further references.

This work has attracted quite a lot of media attention, relatively speaking, for an early career researcher's first research book. I was on BBC Radio Four 'Women's Hour,' which was exciting. The programme brought me wide coverage, profile building and contact from the public, as well as advertising my university, which they liked, of course. A lead article on silence practices for schools (early 2013) in the practitioner PRO magazine of the *Times Educational Supplement* is the first

(Continued)

(Continued)

time I have felt I can really *directly* impact upon many teachers and could widely affect practice in schools. Attention like this prompts me to get continuously informed about how to handle impact engagement.

My advice is make your own luck. Take whatever opportunities come up and enjoy them. Do what feels right and interesting. If it feels wrong, don't. Expect to write media pieces yourself (love journalists!) and so hone a simple sentence structure. Be very careful of your time and keep your mind on serious work. Impact is a fickle friend; always surprising.

REFLECTION POINT

Think back on your career journey so far. Consider the role of chance and serendipity in getting where you are today, with your research and with your career. Consider further ways you could create 'luck' to generate research impact.

'Luck is what happens when preparation meets opportunity.' (Seneca)

'I'm a great believer in luck, and I find the harder I work, the more I have of it.' (Thomas Jefferson)

APPENDIX I

A SPECIAL CASE: RESEARCHER DEVELOPMENT AND THE WORK OF THE IMPACT AND EVALUATION GROUP

CHRISTOPHER WOOD AND PAM DENICOLO

The UK model – an exemplar case study

In the UK, researcher development has been championed by a consolidated collaboration between the Research Councils and Vitae and has become a national agenda. The agenda started in 2002, when Sir Gareth Roberts was commissioned by UK Treasury to produce a report on researchers' development and career prospects. The report was aimed at the 'supply of researchers' in which researcher development is a key route. The resultant 'SET for Success' publication led to substantial investment in researcher development by the Research Councils. The funding, which became widely known as 'Roberts funding', enabled research institutions to instigate or improve on programmes of researcher development. In 2011 Roberts funding ceased but it had been a kick-start and the promotion and support for the development for all early career researchers has become a clear priority for UK research organisations. Thus they are in several respects ahead of the game in relation to the European Framework for Research Careers (2011), especially in relation to the broad profiles of researchers R1, R2 and R3, namely from doctoral to independent researcher levels.

The UK now has an enviable worldwide reputation for its work on the researcher skills agenda, which has played a key role in supporting the academic community by:

- raising the profile of the importance of personal and professional development in researcher training for all stakeholders;
- encouraging the integration of, and opportunities for, personal and professional skills development in research degree programmes;
- promoting and sharing good practice within higher education institutions;
- as a national resource, continuing to innovate, develop and provide exemplar ways of embedding personal and professional development and career management skills.

Following the Research Council funding of researcher development in the UK, there has been a considerable amount of effort placed in evaluating the impact of the investment. Indeed a national impact and evaluation group (IEG) was established to provide a framework for evaluation, and to co-ordinate evaluation activities across the UK (see Chapters 8 and 9). First, some information is presented about the IEG and then about the researcher development context in the UK, followed by a look in more detail at the framework to see how it can help identify when we would expect to see impact in developing researchers.

Impact and evaluation group (previously the Rugby Team)[1]

The mission of the Impact and Evaluation Group is to 'propose a meaningful and workable way of evaluating the effectiveness of skills development in early career researchers'.

The current terms of reference (2008–12) are to:

- inform national and agency policies and practices relating to the evaluation of skills development of researchers;
- provide sector input into shaping a programme to build an evidence base on the effectiveness of developing researchers' skills;
- act as a sector 'sounding board' to Vitae with respect to their engagement in helping to build the evidence base.

Each year it agrees a range of projects, based on the recommendations of the Vitae Policy Forum.

[1]This section is an extract from the Vitae website, which provides much additional information: http://vitae.ac.uk/ieg

The IEG, wherever possible, advises key stakeholders, particularly RCUK and the sector, on the implications for the skills and employability agendas of major initiatives, such as the Bologna process, the European Charter and Code and the Concordat, and future funding and monitoring mechanisms for researcher development.

Researcher development in the UK

Catalysts

It is worth considering the need for appropriate catalysts for agendas designed to generate appropriate impact. A catalyst is something which precipitates fundamental change, in this context a change in the support for researcher development nationwide and in individual institutions. In the case of researcher development, there is no doubt that the QAA Code of Practice (see Quality Assurance Agency, 2004, 2007) was the catalyst that ensured that the recommendations for researcher development (see Roberts, 2001) were rapidly implemented across the higher educational sector. It was useful as the expectations of the desired impact (from the Roberts Report's recommendations) were clear and well communicated.

Within the UK, there has been significant growth in terms of useful data to assess the impact of investment (both in terms of diversity and volume) in the area of researcher development.

Since recommendations were made from government enquiry (see 'SET for Success' report (Roberts, 2001) and final section of this appendix), there has been significant investment in the development of researchers and the richness of this activity is well represented in the various national reports (see Further reading in Chapter 5 for additional details).

Vitae and the impact measure

Vitae, through its sub-group IEG, has examined the impact of researcher training and development, and constructed an impact measure (also see Chapter 8 and final section of Chapter 5). So far, they have been able to detail 120 examples of 'impactful' researcher development, clearly indicating the expansion in researcher development activities within the UK. There is already evidence that researcher development is making an impact in areas such as researcher satisfaction, PhD completion rates and subsequent employability. It is not that this assessment is without its complexities. It is more that the levels of impact expected have been clearly defined and timings anticipated, as we shall see later. It is true that the longer-term impact of researcher development is as difficult to assess as many other types of research, and that the impact may only be apparent after a significant delay (as current early career researchers establish their career credentials), but these time frames are considered and known. By being realistic about when we might expect to see impact we can plan more clearly and make more informed decisions.

It is worth noting in this example that an initial criticism concerning the evaluation of the researcher development agenda was a lack of baseline data (for a discussion of this subject see Chapters 5, 7 and 8, and Kearns and Miller (1997) and Kirkpatrick and Kirkpatrick (2006) referenced in Chapter 5). However, there has been a concerted effort to establish such data, albeit retrospectively. Indeed, an analysis of a sample of 95 of the institutional reports to the UK Research Councils (RCUK, 2010), compared to their respective 2004 outline strategies, provided an increasing clear picture of the distance travelled with the researcher development agenda over the intervening five-year period. More recently, the national Postgraduate Research Experience Survey (PRES) has also confirmed such findings and demonstrates increasing student satisfaction with the results of the agenda in general within the UK. This example is a clear sign of looking for and directing efforts towards achieving impact; this case study was informed by asking the right questions and having a clear agenda, and looking retrospectively for appropriate baseline data (see earlier sections of Chapter 5).

Mapping 'when' onto the Researcher Development Framework

In 2010 Vitae published the Researcher Development Framework (RDF), which articulates the knowledge, behaviours and attributes one would associate with successful researchers. It is a tool to encourage researchers to aspire to excellence through achieving higher levels of personal and professional development.

The RDF was developed by and for researchers, in consultation with academic and non-academic employers. It is a very useful tool when trying to determine when we would see the impact of researcher development as it clearly maps out the attributes expected of researchers at different stages of their research career.

The RDF is structured into four domains which encompass what researchers need to know in order to conduct their research. It also outlines how they should be effective in their approach to research, especially when working with others and contributing to the wider environment.

Each domain is further divided into specific descriptors and associated phases (see Appendix II). The phases seek to capture the knowledge, behaviours and attitudes of competent researchers at different stages of their development.

It this part of the book we will attempt to put a 'time-line' on *when* we would expect to see the impact of researcher development in relation to the RDF structure and descriptors.

In terms of answering the above question it is useful to consider four key stages in researcher development:

- early – postgraduate research students and those at the start of an early research career;
- mid – early research career;
- established – established research career with significant institutional research management responsibilities;
- late – well-established researcher with international reputation and high-level management and financial responsibilities for international research activities.

Table A.1 shows what attributes from the RDF descriptors we might expect to observe compared to the four key stages of researcher development outlined above.

It is hoped that this 'time-line' will aid both researchers and research managers to identify when they would expect to see the impact of researcher development during individual researchers' career spans.

Considering the timing of impact in relation to other measures

Another very useful tool that has emerged in recent years is the 'Impact and Evaluation Group Impact Framework' (IEG-IF). This robust measure was developed 'to identify coherent and transparent ways to evaluate researcher development'. It arose from a number of drivers (see Bromley et al., 2008, Bromley, 2009 and 2010 fully referenced in Chapters 5 and 7), which include requirements for:

i. an evaluation of the appropriateness of the emphasis on skills development;
ii. evidence to present to government and other funding bodies on the impact of their investment;
iii. information to further the enhancement of the quality of the research experience for early career researchers, in line with the QAA recommendations for postgraduates and the concordat for research staff;
iv. assessment of the impact of recent initiatives, particularly the 'Roberts funding' on the employability (or perceived, thereof) of early career researchers.

TABLE A.1 The expected impact/developmental measures outlined in the RDF compared to four key stages of researcher development

Key stages in the development of researchers when 'impact' may become apparent, related to RDF descriptors

Time →

When RDF domain	Early	Mid	Established	Late
Knowledge and intellectual abilities	Subject knowledge Research methods – theoretical and practical Seeking information Academic literacy and numeracy Inquiring mind	Analysing Synthesising Critical thinking Evaluating Problem solving Argument construction Innovation	Intellectual insight	Intellectual risk
Personal effectiveness	Enthusiasm Responsibility Starting/continuation of personal and professional development	Integrity Self-confidence Self-reflection Preparation and prioritisation Commitment to research Time management Career management	Networking Reputation	Perseverance Esteem
Research governance and organisation	Health and safety consideration Ethics Legal requirements IPR and copyright Respect and confidentiality	Appropriate practice Attribution and co-authorship	Managing risk Project planning and delivery Financial management	Sustainability Research strategy Income and funding generation Infrastructure and resources
Engagement influence and impact	Collegiality Team working Equality and diversity	Communication methods Communication media Teaching Collaboration	Publication Public engagement People management Supervision Mentoring	Influence and leadership Enterprise Policy Society and culture Global citizenship

Currently, universities in the UK are encouraged to add examples of using the IEG-IF as part of their reporting to Research Councils. The purpose of conducting these assessments and basing it on the IEG-IF is to:

- support existing methods of evaluation and benchmark such activities;
- compare and contrast such activities with those of other regional and national institutions and competitor organisations;
- aid the HE sector in building a comprehensive evidence base.

The evaluation is conducted through four levels of the IEG-IF:

- Level 0 – Foundations
- Level 1 – Reactions
- Level 2 – Learning
- Level 3 – Behaviour
- Level 4 – Outcomes

Level 0 relates to the investment in infrastructure for training and development activity, such as the development of training programmes. Metrics include: number of training opportunities offered, number of participants and researcher interactions with employers. In short, this acts as a base-line assessment.

Level 1 relates to how participants react to the training and development offered – what their views are. This can also be related to their opinion of the training programme as whole or constituent parts.

Level 2 measures the extent to which participants change attitude, improve knowledge and/or increase skills as a result of attending the training.

Level 3 examines the extent to which participants change their behaviour as a result of attending the training. For example, is the participant now managing their time better as a result of attending a time management workshop? Has the researcher applied what they have learnt?

Finally, Level 4 examines the results of training and development activity. Have changes in behaviour resulted in different outcomes? Has the quality of the research improved? Is there a more highly skilled workforce? Are researchers more employable?

These descriptors of impact assessment are extremely useful (see Chapters 5 to 8) as they allow the continued developmental activity of the researcher to be assessed over time. By understanding what we should expect and when, we can make more informed decisions about what is important to foster in developing researchers and, crucially, when. It is hoped that by combining the impact-level assessments in the IEG-IF with the time-frame provided in Table A.1, a strong guidance 'map' is provided for determining both when to expect impact from researcher development, but also when to foster and encourage the different aspects of development. This should be of use to both researchers and research managers alike.

TABLE A.2 Function of complexity and length of time after development activity, taken from Bromley et al. (2008)

B: Higher complexity, shorter time span	**D: Higher complexity, longer time span**
Personal transformation Increased qualification rates	National, regional or economic growth More creative and entrepreneurial workforce Greater social and cultural capital More highly skilled academics and researchers
A: Lower complexity, shorter time span	**C: Lower complexity, longer time span**
Cognitive growth Greater researcher wellbeing Increased researcher engagement in development opportunities Better-quality research	Growth in start-ups or spin-outs by researchers

Bromley et al. (2008) have also provided another very useful tool which allows us to examine the relationship between time and the complexity of the evidence of impact, in relation to both researcher development and research *per se* (see Table A.2).

As we have seen, measuring impact can be complex. This complexity is further complicated by the progression of time. As time passes by, typically, the more complex the assessment can become as other factors come into play while some of the original ones diminish or disappear as the context changes.

It is important to note that, nevertheless, longer time spans are equally associated with greater researcher competence (see Tables A.1 and A.2).

Table A.2 highlights what impact measures one would expect in relation to short and longer-term time spans.

We hope that you find the contents of Figure A.1 in Appendix II (Summary chart of the RDF) and Tables A.1 and A.2 useful in establishing an individual 'time-frame' of your own for your own personal and professional development. You might want to consider the following when constructing your time-frame: (i) what aspects of your development you need to consider in the future, (ii) when you would expect to see certain behaviour in your research activities, and (iii) how complex some of these actions will be in relation to the diverse nature of your own on-going research activities.

Reference

Bromley, T. and Metcalfe, J. (2008) *The Rugby Team Impact Framework*, Cambridge: Careers Research and Advisory Centre (CRAC).

APPENDIX II

AN ILLUSTRATION OF THE RESEARCHER DEVELOPMENT FRAMEWORK (VITAE)

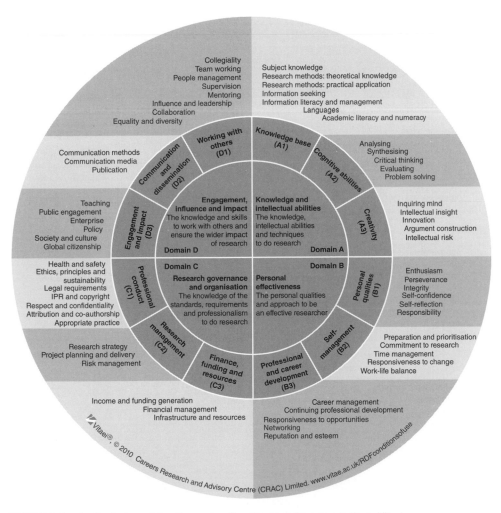

FIGURE A.1   An illustration of the Researcher Development Framework (from Vitae)

Vitae, 2012. Researcher Development Framework – available at http://www.vitae.ac.uk/rdf

APPENDIX III

THE PATHWAYS TO IMPACT FRAMEWORK PROVIDED BY RCUK

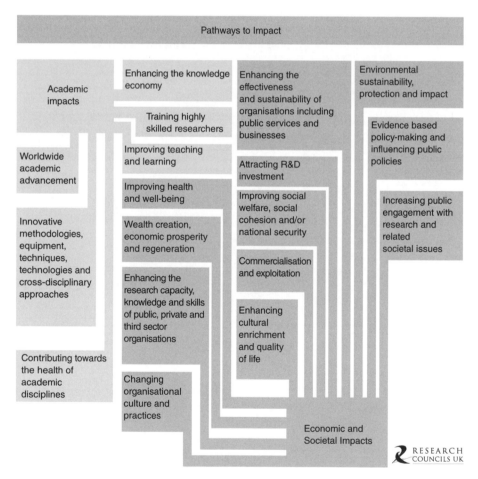

FIGURE A.2 The Pathways to Impact framework provided by RCUK

GLOSSARY

Academic – a person who is engaged with learning, especially in the context of higher education.

Applied research – original investigation undertaken in order to acquire new knowledge. It is, however, directed primarily towards a specific practical aim or objective.

Attribution – acknowledgement of provenance or source.

Basic research – experimental or theoretical work undertaken primarily to acquire new knowledge of the underlying foundation of phenomena and observable facts, without any particular application or use in view.

Baseline data – an initial collection of data which subsequently serves as a basis of comparison for data that is related but collected at a later point.

Baseline environment – a characterisation of the environment before any activity is introduced to attempt to exact change.

Beneficence – the principle of doing good.

Blue-skies research – typically, scientific research in domains where 'real-world' applications are not immediately apparent.

Cohort – a group of students or researchers that is based within the same subject area or discipline.

Congruence – measures that have harmony or are in agreement with each other.

Construction − a phenomenon that does not exist independently of society; rather it is a product of that society. Gender might be considered a construction in terms of expectations of gendered behaviour, whereas a person's sex might be considered a biological state independent of society (debates of nature vs nurture notwithstanding).

Critical realism − a philosophical view about the nature of reality, that there is a stable reality but that our experiences of it are partial. See for example M. Archer, et al. 1998, *Critical Realism: Essential Readings*, London: Routledge.

Curiosity-driven research − like blue-skies research, conducted simply to find out about things with no specific practical output expected or sought.

Doctoral training centre (DTC) − involves a university (or a small number of universities collaborating) in delivering a four-year doctoral training programme to a significant number of PhD students organised into cohorts. Typically, each DTC targets a specific area of research, and emphasises transferable skills training. It is one version of several names for centres of excellence as defined by Research Councils.

Early career researcher (ECR) − a PhD doctoral or postdoctoral researcher who has only been in their field of research for a few years. Typically, in the case of research staff, this equates to those staff in the lower grades of remuneration.

Evaluation map − a table that summaries the key methodological elements of a designed impact study. The evaluation map serves to guide an evaluator in designing an impact study and should be completed before any activity commences.

Experimental development − systematic work, drawing on existing knowledge gained from research and/or practical experience, which is directed to producing new materials, products or devices, to installing new processes, systems and services, or to improving substantially those already produced or installed.

Frascati Manual is a document that formalises the collection and methodology for the survey of research and development at a national level for the Organisation for Economic Co-operation and Development (OECD).

Foucauldian literature − the writings of and commentary on philosopher Michel Foucault's (1926−84) works on power, knowledge and governing.

Impact and evaluation group (IEG) – a sector-wide group within the UK that was brought together to 'propose a meaningful and workable way of evaluating the effectiveness of skills development in early career researchers'. The IEG comprises invited individuals from universities, the Research Councils and Vitae. It was originally called the Rugby Team to mark the location of its first meeting.

Impact factor (IF) – a ratio reflecting the average number of citations of recent articles published in a peer-reviewed journal. IF is intended to complement other 'esteem' measures but is typically used to judge the quality of both the journal and the papers contained therein.

Impactful – having a powerful effect or making a strong impression. Typically, in the case of research, this equates to having a strong effect on behavioural change as a direct result of the research in question.

Impact framework – a document that attempts to summarise the strategic drivers for an impact study, provides context, outlines methodology and summarises potential benefits/impacts of the activity to stakeholders.

Impedance – means to slow or to hinder.

J-eS – Joint electronic submissions is the first point of contact for grant services with the Research Councils.

Knowledge transfer/knowledge exchange – the systems and processes by which a two-way flow of people or ideas is achieved between the research environment and non-academic organisations, for mutual benefit. Non-academic organisations may include businesses, NGOs, public sector organisations or other scientists.

Logic diagram – the logical mechanism through which the desired outcomes and impacts of designed activity are expected to be realised.

Metrics – measurable, quantitative phenomena collected in the monitoring of organisational performance (also known as key performance indicators). Businesses might collect metrics on sales, customer satisfaction or staff turnover to compare performance over seasons or years.

Non-maleficence – the principle of causing no harm.

Paradigm – a basic set of beliefs that guide action, including the questions asked or hypotheses made, and include the researcher's epistemological, ontological and methodological premises.

Prospective – future.

Proxy – a measured variable used to infer the value of a variable of interest.

Postgraduate Research Experience Survey (PRES) – a UK-wide survey that is made available by the higher education authority to all higher education Institutes with postgraduate researchers. PRES is designed to help institutions enhance the quality of postgraduate research degree provision by collecting feedback from current postgraduate researchers.

Product – a tangible article that is designed and manufactured for sale.

Quality Assurance Agency (QAA) – a UK independent body to safeguard quality and standards in UK universities and colleges.

Research and experimental development (R&D) – creative work undertaken on a systematic basis in order to increase the stock of knowledge, including knowledge of humanity, culture and society, and the use of this stock of knowledge to devise new applications (OECD, 2002: 31).

Research Councils UK (RCUK) – responsible for investing public money in research in the UK. Sir Gareth Roberts' report published in April 2002 covered the supply of science, technology, engineering and mathematics skills throughout the education system. He made several recommendations relating directly to postgraduate researchers and research staff.

Research Excellence Framework (REF) – the successor of the Research Assessment Exercise (RAE), a process of assessing the quality of research in universities in the UK through peer review panels. Outcomes of the RAE were used to decide allocations of research funding from the higher education funding councils as opposed to the Research Councils which form the other source of research funding in the 'dual-support system'.

Research Quality Framework (RQF) – a best practice framework in Australia for assessing research quality and the impact of research.

Retrospective – looking back to the past.

Risk – the potential that an activity will lead to an undesirable outcome, or that an unfavourable event will occur, usually measured against the dimensions of likelihood and impact.

Royal Charter – a formal document issued by the Crown, granting rights to an individual or organisation in perpetuity.

Rugby Team Impact Framework – the impact framework developed by the UK researcher training and development sector. The development of the framework was led by the Impact and Evaluation Group (IEG – see glossary entry), which was formerly known as the 'Rugby Team' because its first meeting was held in the UK town of Rugby.

Service – the act of helping, supporting, advising or doing work for a third party.

SET for Success – a report by Sir Gareth Roberts which catalysed change in the way researchers are supported in higher education.

Skills, generic and transferable – abilities that are useful within a range of circumstances, including a range of jobs, which once acquired in one context might be readily amended to fit in another situation.

Stakeholder – a person or organisation with a legitimate interest in an organisation's actions.

Taxonomy – the conception, naming and classification of groups of information.

Third sector – the sphere of activity undertaken by organisations that are involved with activities that are not for profit.

INDEX